Carry on, teachers!
representations of the
teaching profession in
screen culture

Carry on, teachers!
representations of the teaching profession in screen culture

Susan Ellsmore

Trentham Books
Stoke on Trent, UK and Sterling, USA

Trentham Books Limited
Westview House   22883 Quicksilver Drive
734 London Road   Sterling
Oakhill   VA 20166-2012
Stoke on Trent   USA
Staffordshire
England ST4 5NP

First published 2005

British Library Cataloguing-in-Publication Data
A catalogue record for this book is available from the British Library

Cover photograph: © Canal + Image UK Ltd.

ISBN-13: 978-1-85856-359-6
ISBN-10: 1-85856-359-3

Designed and typeset by Trentham Print Design Ltd, Chester and printed in Great Britain by Cromwell Press Ltd, Trowbridge.

Acknowledgements

I would like to thank the following people for their support in the production of this book: All the teachers who gave up time to watch and respond to a selection of films and/or television programmes: John, Linda, Sue, Monique, Sue, Harry, Bob, Frank, Trish, Karen, Matt, Sue, Lee, Carey, Katie, Val, Lucy, Melanie, Chrissy, Zoe, Freya, Béatrice, Paul and especially to Julie Cleminson for organising the members of the sample based near her.

Judith Ranger for word processing the manuscript, and Enid Nixon for proof reading it.

Gillian Klein for her help and advice throughout the writing process, and Barbara Wiggins of Trentham Books and John Stipling of Trentham Print Design.

Ian Bennett, Paddie Collyer, David Gauntlett, Mike Richards, Dennis Wardleworth, my colleagues and year 13 students at school, my colleagues at university, and staff at the British Film Institute Stills Department.

Brian Ellsmore for his patience and encouragement, to whom this book is dedicated.

Introduction

I am sitting in the local cinema on a summer's afternoon in 2004, watching *Mona Lisa Smile*. It's the latest film about a charismatic teacher who inspires her students to 'seize the day', as John Keating, another *reel* charismatic teacher, would have put it. As the plot unfolds, other films about charismatic teachers come to mind – Mr Chips and his disastrous first encounter with the boys of Brookfield School; Glenn Holland, who thought that becoming a teacher would give him time to write his opus; Jean Brodie who, on the surface, appeared to be giving her girls the sort of education which went beyond the official curriculum – and the many others you will meet in this book.

As the 'educator-hero' (Farber and Holm, 1994: 153) and 'people of substance' (von Gunden, 1990: 170) charismatic teachers are capable of inspiring their students as no other member of staff can. At the simplest level of storyline, charismatic teachers are 'in the business of saving children' (Ayers, 2001: 201). They have the ability to attract and inspire the loyalty and admiration of their students. They form a special relationship with a group of students with whom they operate in isolation to a greater or lesser degree and are 'willing to do right by them at great personal cost' (Dalton, 1999: 31). The assumption in many charismatic teacher films is that the only figure in the school who understands what makes these students tick is the go-it-alone maverick.

In the *Times Educational Supplement* (16/07/99) columnist Libby Purves wrote about her reaction to *Hope and Glory*, a television drama series featuring Lenny Henry as the saviour superhead of a failing secondary school. The programme made her reflect on 'the changes in the ways schools are portrayed in filmed fiction'. She offered this challenge to her readers: 'Someone should write a proper thesis: fictional teachers from Wackford Squeers to Ian George (Lenny Henry) and what they tell us.' Thanks to my former headteacher, who believed I was mad enough to undertake a PhD, not only was I writing that thesis, I was also writing about what teachers – those who are represented – tell us about those texts.

And I *was* mad – in more than one sense of the word. I was angry at what was being done to the teaching profession, the 'demonisation of' (Nicoll, *G2*, 19/06/96), or – as Mike Baker, Education Correspondent for the BBC, puts it the 'demolition job' on (2000b: 34) – the teaching profession by the negative news coverage of the print and broadcast media. Education has become a sexy subject, and what happens in schools is now open to greater public scrutiny than ever before. The growth in education journalism is irrevocably linked to the plethora of government initiatives, the Thatcherite reforms of the 1980s, which can be seen as a process of deprofessionalisation, questioning teacher autonomy over what was taught in schools. Day cites the last 20 years as 'years of survival, rather than development' (2000: 101) for the teaching profession. Teachers work in a very different educational landscape to that of a generation ago, finding it increasingly hard to put their own ideas about teaching into practice. 'The integrity of living one's life according to the calling of one's occupation is now denied' (Woods *et al*, cited by Ball, 1999: 103).

With hindsight, I can see it was writing my PhD thesis that kept me in the classroom. Not only was it my continuing professional development, it was also a cathartic experience which helped me to understand just how the profession I came into over 20 years ago had changed so radically. And, dare I say it, it was fun – it was not in line with other mainstream educational research. Now I have tried to change that thesis into a book which I hope will be of some relevance to practising teachers, to teachers-in-training, to those thinking of joining the profession – indeed, to anyone who has ever been to school.

From the *reel* world of teaching, Jones' (1999) exploration of *Kes* and *Grange Hill* shows that popular texts provide a picture of contemporary educational issues, but they also represent education in a style which assumes the need to handle it in ways that will educate – as well as entertain – an audience. The recommissioning of *Hope and Glory* after its first series is a good example of the BBC's drive to strengthen its focus on and commitment to educational issues (*Broadcast*, July 9, 1999). According to Giroux (2002: 15), 'Film constitutes a powerful force for shaping public memory, hope, popular consciousness, and social agency and as such invites people into a broader public conversation'.

Mitchell and Weber (1999) claim that, in spite of their imperfections, films have relevance for teachers at any stage in their professional lives because they can enhance understanding of an individual's practice and school context. As an unconventional source of educational theory, the representation of teachers in screen culture could play a role in initial teacher training; a number of commentators chart the demise of educational theory during the last 30 years, as the New Right have questioned the need for any theoretical content in teacher training courses. Practical competence in teaching is what is now emphasised, and this can best be achieved via school-based training; knowledge of educational disciplines provides nothing for teachers-in-training which they can pass on to students when they start teaching. However, McLelland (1996) argues that teachers ignore the importance of educational theory at their peril, as the social, learning and behavioural problems students bring into the classroom cannot be properly tackled without a theoretical foundation.

Nonetheless, the majority of teachers appear to have little time for philosophical dialogue based on education theory, and initial teacher training programmes are not taken seriously. 'The study of philosophy, psychology, sociology and history of education ... result(s) in a few, a very few, students adopting a more understanding approach to children, parents and even their colleagues' (Rée, cited by Mardle and Walker 1980: 110):

> [Teachers] do not value education theory as a systematic, coherent, and authoritative body of knowledge and insights that might have some relevance for their classroom practice. They [reject] it in their initial training, and they [continue] to have little acquaintance with it and make little use of it in their current practice. Few teachers [claim]

to have much interest in contemporary writings on education. (Hargreaves 1984: 248)

So if, as teachers maintain, the articles in educational journals are out of touch with the everyday experiences of life in schools, an alternative source of educational theory might be the charismatic teacher film. 'Perhaps a training college could see film as a method of exploring the truth of relationships in school – it might be more productive than discussing targets and lesson plans' (Maclaren, *Times Educational Supplement*, 01/01/99).

> It is a matter of no small import to recognize that one brief showing of the motion picture *Stand and Deliver* on public television (and later rebroadcast on commercial television) was seen by three to four million people while the combined yearly circulation of the top 25 professional education journals are read by a little more than 250,000 practitioners. (Ulrich's Yearbook, 1991-1992, cited by Underwood 1992: 92)

Screen culture provides resources which can be plundered and exploited as a source of educational theory for both practising teachers and teachers-in-training as a means of questioning and reflecting on their work. Moore (2004: 63) sees the purpose of such images as to 'be criticised and deconstructed in the PGCE seminar room, and consideration given, perhaps, to other models of good teaching that may be conspicuously absent from such media representations'. Weber and Mitchell (1995) are more positive when they suggest that films provide an informal curriculum or alternative Faculty of Education for those who wish to become teachers. They cite the example of the impact of *To Sir, With Love* on one of the authors:

> I remember identifying with Sir as he battled with cynical teachers, prejudice and ignorance, ultimately rejecting a much more prestigious career as an engineer for the love of teaching, for the love of children. Romantic!? Heady stuff?! Prior to seeing the movie, I had never even considered a career in teaching, but I did not forget that film. It lingered somewhere in the sedimentary collage of images that form the inchoate, primary material for thinking and feeling. (p133)

Giroux (1993, 1997, 2002) is another educationalist who has utilised popular culture as part of his course for undergraduate teachers-in-training. He believes that texts such as films should be examined as serious sources of pedagogical knowledge, giving those who train teachers opportunities to reflect on the nature of educational theory and practice and what it means for twentieth-first century initial teacher training:

> Films provided me with a pedagogical tool for offering students alternative views of the world. Of course, films not only challenged print culture as the only viable source of knowledge, they were attractive cultural texts for students because they were not entirely contaminated by the logic of formal schooling. As a young high school teacher, I too was attracted to films as a way of challenging the constraints imposed by the rigidity of the text-based curriculum. (Giroux, 2002: 3)

To a certain extent the charismatic teacher film draws on real life experiences because everyone who works in the *reel* world – actors, screenplay writers, directors – will have been to school. Full-time education in Britain is a legal requirement between the ages of five and sixteen; Squires (1999) points out that very few societal experiences are compulsory for so long. This means that everyone has extensive experience of being taught, so has some ideas about how teaching should be. It is inevitable that a number of these ideas will find their way into the charismatic teacher film: 'I think there must be something universal about the childhood experience of a beloved and influential teacher' (Spark, *Radio Times*, 31 July-6 August, 2004).

Can teacher readings of film representations be linked with their everyday construction of teacher performance? And do films indeed offer space for reflecting on professional change and development? Members of the teaching profession could argue the charismatic teacher film oversimplifies real experience, resulting in a poor representation of teaching culture. Dickinson (*Sight and Sound*, February 2000: 50) sums up audience expectations of the basic plot of the charismatic teacher film: 'we anticipate a protagonist's battle and an inevitable triumph over an assembly of doubting Thomases'. In her review of *Dangerous Minds* (*Sight and Sound*, January 1996: 37), Francke envisages the point of view of real world teachers:

> Apart from Pfeiffer's inability to convince as a teacher, anyone who has ever taught professionally will find much else to scoff at. Lou-Anne has an ever-full private purse out of which she subsidises her

charges' educational needs, whether with the copious photocopies that she hands out or with fiscally damaging treats (day trips for the class en masse, swanky dinners for teachers' pets). (p37)

Because these films can seem patronising in their portrayal of teachers, they may marginalise people in the profession. With the real world problems missing from the picture, the everyday experiences of teachers may be seen as frustrating and demoralising when compared with the *reel* world, where schools are portrayed as somewhere more exciting to work. '[Representations] blur or blot out entirely the real conditions of teachers' daily lives, diminishing the different and extraordinarily varied and complex work of teachers' (Keroes 1999: 135). Walters (1988) writes about teachers' reactions to Jaime Escalante in *Stand and Deliver*:

> It might sound unpromising, but the picture gets genuine drama out of classroom battles and examination nerves. ... For the most part, we readily believe that this slouched, balding, unimpressive figure can catch the interest and imagination of the kids. ... I saw the film with an audience of teachers, and most left looking faintly depressed – partly, I suspect, because it puts so much importance on a single, charismatic individual. (*Listener*: 39)

Films and television programmes are made to entertain and it is therefore tempting to regard them as texts which have nothing to do with teachers or the reality of schooling (Maclaren, *Times Educational Supplement*, 01/01/99). Although popular film may be considered culturally inferior to art and literature, and likewise the pleasure gained from it, this does not mean that film should be ignored as being unworthy of academic attention (Stacey, 1994).

Indeed, *Mr Holland's Opus* attracted significant political attention when it was mentioned in debates on arts education in the House of Representatives during the first fortnight of its release (Cornwell, *Times Educational Supplement*, 10/05/96). Albert Shanker, president of the American Federation of Teachers, claimed it had 'special power for people who know something about the teaching life'. And Lois Tinson, president of the California Teachers' Association, noted: 'Since the opening of *Mr Holland's Opus*, a day does not pass without my hearing praise of this wonderful film. Teachers love it ... thank you for reminding us all of the joys of shaping the lives of students.' Bill

Buchanan likewise reinforced the significance of film to entertain and educate:

> The intention of this film was to make people think about their teachers and the great things they do, and to acknowledge all those people who influenced their lives. And it has done that. Newspapers across the country are running articles about great teachers. I have numerous letters from people who have looked up their teachers and thanked them. So, *Mr Holland's Opus* has been particularly satisfying on that level. I believe we have a responsibility when we work in popular culture to try and make things better. (Duncan, *Creative Screenwriting*, Summer 1996: 40)

Although Schwartz (1960) claims that 'at first glance, the educator's portrayal in literature does not suggest an interesting, exciting, or glamorous character for a major role in a feature motion picture' (p82), according to Farber, Provenzo and Holm (1994: 14) images of teachers struggling with 'disabling conditions' provide powerful and comforting representations. The charismatic teacher film may help recharge real world teachers' emotional batteries because their story-lines seem to offer some solution to an individual's concerns. It is not uncommon for people to turn to fiction to find examples of the same sorts of problems they face in their daily lives in order that they, through identification with a fictional character's experience, can work through and resolve their real life dilemmas (Taylor, 1989).

In an age of visual culture, it can be asserted that films can be important for image-based research as historical documents (Andrew, 1998) in the same way that political cartoons 'are evidence which can be used to reconstruct a social history of education as it is represented in public discourse' (Warburton, 1998: 261). Drawing on their narrative role, the use of the charismatic teacher film can be likened to Richard Gordon's Doctor stories about the medical profession. Such films 'can give unique insights. ... Novels can also be used as a topic of study in themselves, quite apart from their value as data to be used in studies of the social worlds which they describe' (McNeill, 1990: 111).

My selection of films and television programmes from screen culture involved a number of theoretical and practical decisions. It would be impossible to view everything produced, whether in its totality or in the form of extracts. As Andrew (1998: 181) explains: 'The social historian consults the fullest archive available for the topic, from which a few fiction films are selected as the richest examples and most indicative sources of indirect evidence.' A major factor for inclusion was that aspects of teachers' professional lives were realistically represented in screen culture and as closely related as possible to real life practices.

The film sample chosen focused on a teacher or teachers as the main character, rather than as what Loukides and Fuller (1990: 3) term 'stock characters' who play some supporting role, or who appear in the text as part of the background cultural setting for the main action of the film. With the teacher in the starring role, this meant that the sample from screen culture included texts where the storyline centred around the teacher rather that the student. The director of *Blackboard Jungle*, Richard Brooks, comments:

> There were many pictures about juvenile delinquency immediately following this one because of its success. But I started off to make a picture about a teacher, not about juvenile delinquency at all. If you see the picture again, watch how the spokes of the wheel keep on coming back to what the teacher is about. (Cameron *et al*, *Movie*, April 1965: 6)

Real life teachers work in a variety of educational institutions. The films and television programmes I chose are set in the secondary sector of education, rather than the primary or higher or special sectors – although Jean Brodie has contact with students in the junior department of her school. Furthermore, the texts largely represent the state rather than the private system, the exceptions being *Good-bye, Mr. Chips, The Prime of Miss Jean Brodie, Dead Poets Society*, and *Mona Lisa Smile*.

Sixteen films – eight of them British – and three British television programmes were chosen to make up the screen culture sample discussed in this book (see opposite).

Two samples of secondary school teachers volunteered to watch a selection of teacher texts. The first sample of seventeen teachers watched six films. Another group of thirteen teachers viewed one episode from each of the first two series of Channel 4's *Teachers*. The teachers were asked to make a written response about their reception of each film and television episode, using a questionnaire as a frame-

Film/TV	Year	Main Character
Goodbye, Mr. Chips	1939	Charles Chipping
Blackboard Jungle	1955	Richard Dadier
It's Great To Be Young	1956	Mr Dingle
Carry On Teacher	1959	Mr Wakefield and ensemble
Spare the Rod	1961	John Saunders
To Sir, With Love	1967	Mark Thackeray
The Prime of Miss Jean Brodie	1969	Jean Brodie
Please Sir!	1971	Bernard Hedges
Clockwise	1986	Brian Stimpson
Stand and Deliver	1988	Jaime Escalante
Dead Poets Society	1989	John Keating
Dangerous Minds	1995	LouAnne Johnson
Hearts and Minds	1995	Drew McKenzie
Mr Holland's Opus	1995	Glenn Holland
To Sir, With Love 2	1996	Mark Thackeray
187	1997	Trevor Garfield
Hope and Glory	1999	Ian George
Teachers	2001 onwards	Simon Casey
Mona Lisa Smile	2003	Katherine Watson

work. The knowledge gained from audience reception of texts must be treated with caution, because the complexity of the viewing context, coupled with the social position of the individual viewer, impinges on reception of media content. The multi-dimensional quality of the viewing process means that viewers will respond to a media text in different ways. The significance of what is watched may have little or no influence, as some messages may be ignored, some interpreted in unexpected ways, and some accepted totally. The individual will also adopt different viewing habits under different circumstances.

Before members of the audience can assess the realism of a representation, they need to be familiar with those aspects of 'real life' the film or television programme is referring to. According to their experience and construction of reality there will be differences in how each person receives a text, and how they perceive the overlap between real and *reel* life. Real life teachers are ideally situated to assess the realism of their *reel* life counterparts – as general film viewers *and* teachers they bring original insights. Both Morley's (1980) and Kuhn's (1995) research show how a professional reading of a text compares with an amateur one, thus identifying that individuals' reading positions are at least partially socially determined. Bringing different kinds of prior knowledge and experience to a text makes people more or less 'culturally competent' (Morley 1992: 128). So teachers are bound to be critical readers of films about teaching.

The insights gained from the teacher samples into teacher representations in screen culture and their reception and relevance to professional development must be recognised as being grounded in a complexity of variables which a discursive paradigm of audience reception recognises. For example, a Head of Year is more directly involved in pastoral care than a Head of Department, and will therefore bring more managerial experience of the pastoral role to reading the films. Likewise, the type of school the people in the teacher samples have worked in will colour their interpretation of *reel* world portrayals of classrooms and staffrooms. For the six teachers who took part in both parts of the study, promotion, a new job in a new school – simply more years in the teaching profession – will have affected their responses to teacher representations in screen culture.

But how are the real world insights of all those who took part in this study dealt with? When starting analysis, it is important to acknowledge the complexity of the process of re-presenting individual responses and the overlap or disagreement between them. Plummer (1990) identifies an analytical spectrum, bounded at one end by the extent to which the author imposes her own understanding on that of the respondent, and at the other by the extent to which the latter's account is 'allowed' to stand in its 'purest' form with minimal intervention from the author. The author positions herself somewhere between these two ends, depending on how she imposes analytical devices on the responses. This locates the philosophy of the author at a point where a 'story' is imposed on the responses, and the story is enriched by quotes from members of the teacher samples.

But before telling the story, the first chapter maps the changes in the teaching profession since the second world war up to the mid-1990s, so shedding light on the cultural background of the teaching profession. The two most significant Education Acts of the twentieth century, those implemented by Rab Butler in 1944 and Kenneth Baker in 1988, are studied as events that might have influenced four British films which constitute the first part of a four-fold typology of the charismatic teacher film, that of the eccentric charismatic teacher. This historical perspective is continued in chapter two, where the screen culture focus shifts to television and how three drama series have mirrored change and development in the teaching profession as it moved into the twentieth-first century under two successive New Labour governments. Chapter three focuses on two *reel* world teachers who work in pleasant school settings, and who put their respective schools and students at the centre of their personal and professional lives for over 30 years. The second element of the four-fold typology, the enduring charismatic teacher film, provides a complete picture of the teaching life cycle, and reflects a vocational life course which is fast disappearing. The chapter also looks at government initiatives to encourage recruitment to and retention within the teaching profession.

Chapter four maps the development of the charismatic teacher film since the second world war up to the present day via ten films. Four of these, based on real life stories about teachers working in inner city school settings, constitute the third part of the four-fold typology, the resilient charismatic teacher. Members of the first teacher sample make their responses to the relationships formed between the main characters and their students and colleagues, and the reality of these films in chapter five. The last chapter considers the final element of the four-fold typology, the romantic charismatic teacher film, together with the rest of the responses from the first teacher sample. It concludes with Channel 4's *Teachers* and the second teacher sample's responses to the series.

Chapter 1

The British comedy film introduces eccentric charismatic teachers and their relationships with their recalcitrant students. It also maps the development of the secondary school after the second world war, which set in motion a period of intense professional change (see Hargreaves, 2000). As historical documents, all films preserve visual and narrative information, and although not produced out of an educational culture, they supply evidence about how the teaching profession changes. This despite the fact that 'the history of education has been virtually expunged from teacher education, leaving teachers-in-training unable to engage with the history of their own profession' (McCulloch, *Times Educational Supplement*, 29/10/04). The analysis of the films sheds light on the cultural background of members of both teacher samples, who trained and worked in schools from the late 1960s onwards, and helps provide the professional context of their responses to charismatic teacher films.

In parodying and satirising the education system in its various forms – state and private, tri-partite and comprehensive – British comedy films deal with the wider historical and organisational contexts in which teachers work. Hargreaves (2000) charts the development of teacher professionalism through four phases. Beginning with the 1944 Education Act and the creation of the tri-partite system, what he terms 'the pre-professional age' (p153) followed traditional patterns of chalk and talk. Fundamental problems of discipline and order were at its core. We see teaching and learning styles within the traditional culture of the grammar and secondary modern schools in *It's Great To Be Young* (1956) and *Carry On Teacher* (1959) respectively.

The mid-1960s to the early 1970s saw the birth of the comprehensive school system, and the development of 'the age of the autonomous professional' (Hargreaves, 2000: 153). Teacher status and innovation was at its height with respect to both curriculum and pastoral development, and the latter is reflected in the film, *Please Sir!* (1971). The growth of the comprehensive system and increased complexity of schooling from the late 1970s onwards saw the rise of 'the age of the collegial professional' (*ibid*). *Clockwise* (1986) mirrors the more successful aspects of a comprehensive school system which had found its feet by the mid-1980s. The last of the three films featuring representations of *reel* colleagues either at the chalkface or at senior management level was released two years before the 1988 Education Reform Act.

The final phase Hargreaves discussed, that of the post- (or post-modern) professional, concludes this chapter, together with a brief overview of one of the Conservative government's most controversial initiatives, the creation of the Office for Standards in Education, Ofsted.

The age of the pre-professional

The tri-partite organisation of state schools was founded via the 1944 (Butler) Act. The state system he inherited consisted of the elementary school, offering compulsory free education to the majority of the school population from the age of five to fourteen. A minority of children, selected by examination at eleven, went on to take up special scholarship places in local authority secondary schools, many of which had been modelled on the independent grammar schools in the private sector.

After the second world war, the development of the Welfare State meant that schooling was extended on a wider basis. The expansion of the state system saw the birth of the primary and secondary sectors, the latter offering three types of education for three 'types' of child: the academic, the vocational and the practical. It is rarely acknowledged that the 1944 Act allowed for these three types of education to be offered under the one roof of the multilateral or common, i.e. comprehensive school, because the tri-partite system became the norm.

The grammar school was the top of this tri-partite system, providing an academic education for students interested in learning for learning's sake. Grammar schools would produce the future professionals and people suited to management level administrative and business positions. Secondly, there was the technical school, offering a vocational education for students interested in applied science and/or the arts. Because little money was made available to education in the wake of the second world war, only 2 per cent of the population attended such schools, and despite the sustained campaign by the *Times Educational Supplement* to promote the development of such schools, new technical schools were only built in special cases (Lowe, 1988).

Lastly, there was the modern school, providing a practical education for students who were not being prepared for any specific job or occupation. It was believed that they would benefit from an integrated approach to subjects – the sciences, the arts and the humanities – underpinned by a gender-specific practical curriculum. Whichever school students found themselves in, the main concern for teachers was order and control, with precious little consideration for teaching and learning styles beyond a didactic chalk and talk approach.

As Desforges (1995) points out, large numbers of children in overcrowded classrooms do not create a productive learning environment. Furthermore, many secondary school age students may not want to be in school; they have no interest in the curriculum, and a great deal of the material they are taught is never justified to them. When the nature of the environment is combined with that of the students, Desforges continues, it is not surprising that students finding themselves in a boring and meaningless situation will do something to disrupt lessons.

This device is well-utilised in the eccentric charismatic teacher films set in secondary schools. One of the first films to be made about the newly-constructed tri-partite state system featured a grammar school was the musical comedy *It's Great To Be Young*. With only the top 16 per cent of the secondary school population in grammar schools, this may have seemed an odd choice, but earlier films had largely featured schools in the private sector of education, for example, Frank

Launder and Sidney Gilliat's *The Happiest Days of Your Life*, and the *St Trinians* series.

True to the *reel* world's commitment to monitoring and mirroring social change, the cinema turned its attention away from the portrayal of public schools at around this time (Aldgate and Richards, 1999). The country grammar school in *It's Great To Be Young*, Angel Hill, is clearly a descendant of the public school tradition: extensive buildings and immaculate grounds are populated by polite students from middle-class backgrounds wearing the school uniform (Aldgate and Richards, 1999). Following the theme of student rebellion established by *Blackboard Jungle*, the 'Angels' only link with juvenile delinquency is their desire to play jazz. The film explores the compromise between academic and non-academic achievement, and this persists in contemporary ideology in the concern about privileging league tables over extra-curricular activities.

The first day of the summer term at Angel Hill Co-Educational Grammar School is also the first day in post for the new headteacher, Mr Frome. Welcomed in Assembly by an energetic performance by the school orchestra under the leadership of Mr Dingle, it is not long before Mr Frome makes it clear that he favours the emphasis on academic work rather than such extra-curricular activities as music and sport.

However, Mr Dingle is not of the same opinion and he tells the headteacher: 'Well, I think there's too much emphasis on dates and facts and figures – that's what's wrong with modern schooling'. It is not his ideology to curtail extra-curricular activities in favour of results, and he has entered the school orchestra in the National Festival of School Orchestras. In need of some new musical instruments for the festival, they resort to busking to raise money. Predictably, when their activities come to the attention of the headteacher, he makes them stop. As a last resort, Mr Dingle pays for the instruments himself, taking another job playing the piano in the local pub – at least he gets free beer for his labours! Not one to be crossed, the headteacher has the instruments locked away, so Mr Dingle has to drop a hint to his students about how to get into the cupboard. Having taken the hint, the students get themselves a set of duplicate keys, but a colleague of Mr Dingle's then tells the headteacher, with the result that Mr Dingle is forced to resign for disobedience.

The students go on strike, and stage a series of protests for the re-instatement of their beloved teacher. Staff and students gathered for Assembly are showered with pieces of paper proclaiming 'We Want Dingle' dropped through the skylight in the roof. At the end of his tether, the headteacher cuts the term short by three days, convinced that the long summer break will clear the matter up. But the students do not give up so easily: they retaliate by barricading themselves in the gym.

The headteacher goes to see Mr Dingle, admits that he has been at fault and that he realises he has not done his job well. Now it looks as if he should resign. Mr Dingle is shamed into action by these words, and together they go to talk to the students. Mr Dingle explains that he was wrong to breach the school's disciplinary code in defying the headteacher. He even tries to persuade the students that he does not want to teach at the school anyway. The headteacher is obviously touched by Mr Dingle's words, and he backs down. So Mr Dingle is re-instated, the headteacher does not lose face, and the school orchestra is saved. According to the review in *To-day's Cinema* (31/05/56), 'Dingle must have rare qualities as a teacher to inspire such devoted if misguided loyalty' (p12).

Another tactic employed by the Angels during their campaign was to sabotage the visit of a school inspector. School inspection (the contemporary state of which is discussed later on in this chapter) and undermining its success also underpins the storyline in the film *Carry On Teacher*, which moves even further away from the public school system. For the majority of the secondary school age population, the secondary modern school was the type of education they experienced, and the school which features in this film would be familiar to over 80 per cent of its potential audience. The early films in the *Carry On* series focused on the institutions which grew out of the Welfare State which attempted to conquer five perceived giant evils in society: squalor, disease, ignorance, idleness and want. After *Carry On Sergeant*, the introduction of a National Health Service to fight disease was portrayed in *Carry On Nurse*, the second in the series, and the development of the education system to combat ignorance in the third, *Carry On Teacher.*

Carry On Teacher belongs to the canon of work by Norman Hudis. Unlike Talbot Rothwell, who relied on the thinnest of storylines supplemented by plenty of jokes, Hudis went for a sentimental ending (Bright and Ross, 2000), which *Carry On Teacher* arguably provides. The familiar faces were led by Ted Ray as the acting headteacher, Mr Wakefield, who was described in the *Financial Times* (Robinson, 07/09/59) as a 'kind of Mr Chips', a reference to an earlier 'classic' teacher film:

> His staff is composed mainly of eccentric characters who are nicely assorted and all have plenty of 'fat' without being on the screen long enough to become tedious. There's Kenneth Connor giving a fine performance as a nervous science master, Kenneth Williams and Charles Hawtrey, as a couple of precious masters in charge of literature and music [sic] respectively; Hattie Jaques as the formidable mistress who wages war on the saboteurs, and Joan Sims in her usual inimitable form as a games mistress. (*Variety*, 02/09/59)

These *reel* world teachers mirror the variety of ideologies held by their counterparts in the real world. Kenneth Connor is Mr Adams, whose enthusiasm for his subject implies the frustrated scientist who may well have settled for teaching as a second choice of career. As Mr Bean ('our Malcolm Sargeant of Maudlin Street'), Charles Hawtrey is not only the French and Music teacher but also an amateur musician, combining teaching and composing his own work, and finding an outlet for its performance via school productions. Mr Milton, the English teacher played by Kenneth Williams, represents the teachers who stress the importance of social-psychological theories of learning, then in their infancy, which would become the basis of the later Bachelor of Education (BEd) degree. Opposed to such ideas is Miss Allcock, played by Joan Sims, who has no time for theoretical input. She claims to know children from working practically with them – akin to those professionals who believe teaching is best learnt in the thick of the classroom. Also against the ideas of Mr Milton is the deputy head Miss Short, played by Hattie Jaques, who does not believe in sparing the rod to save the child: firm discipline is the answer to all problems. With these diverse characterisations, *Carry On Teacher* particularly plays to audience memories of their own real world teachers as 'a motley collection of individuals':

> Our teachers' peculiarities of appearance, speech and action, their praise and encouragement, their anger and punishments, all these retain a curious clarity and freshness in our memories of life at school. (Hargreaves, 1982: 192)

As acting headteacher, Mr Wakefield is in the process of applying for a permanent headteacher's post at a brand new school. He calls the staff together to inform them that Mauldin Street will shortly have a visit from the Ministry of Education and that if he is to stand any chance of getting the post he is applying for, he must prove that he is in control of both the students and the staff.

The visitors arrive, and during their tour of the school an orchestrated student campaign of mishaps swings into action. In Music, the leg of the piano collapses; in Physical Education, the gym teacher's shorts split; in English, the teacher has to field an embarrassing question and answer session about the more intimate details missing from the school's edition of Shakespeare's *Romeo and Juliet*; and in Science, a rocket which has been tampered with is accidentally launched and goes through the classroom roof. Having sabotaged the classrooms, the students change tack and, lulling the staff into a false sense of security, continue their campaign by attacking the staffroom. The culmination of the operation is the school play, and this collapses, unsurprisingly, in a shambles.

As the film develops, the audience see the tables turned on teachers such as those who once controlled them and watch the Maudlin Street staff being subjected to various humiliations. However, the story is resolved with a tear-jerking ending when the boys who have wreaked havoc during the inspection week are rounded up and taken to the headteacher's study on the last day of term. As Mr Wakefield prepares to cane them, one of the girl ringleaders and the deputy head intervene, offering an explanation for the week's events. Miss Short takes up the story:

> Mr Wakefield, these children discovered you were planning to leave. They don't want you to leave – it's as simple as that. They feel, as does the entire school, that Maudlin Street wouldn't be the same without you. They thought of setting up a petition, but decided that wasn't certain to succeed. Besides, such an action was considered by them to be soft – not the Maudlin Street way. So, with all the circumstances

in their favour, they decided to make sure you would never obtain a post anywhere else and launched their campaign to that end, with the whole school behind them. You may wish to proceed with punishing these boys. Personally, I would count my years in the profession well spent if they do half as much to make me stay among them.

Thus the charismatic Mr Wakefield inspires loyalty and admiration in both his students and staff, and this is reinforced by the deputy head's words. But such happy endings for students and staff were not characteristic of real life in secondary modern schools. In theory, the grammar, technical and secondary modern schools were to be regarded as equivalent to one another, and therefore to be accorded equal respect by students, parents and the local community. But parity of esteem was soon exposed as unrealistic: in time, the idea that three types of child could be identified for three types of school became unacceptable. Another system of schooling appeared on the horizon, ripe for parody. According to Simon (1994), this became the most controversial institution in the history of the English education system: the comprehensive school.

The age of the autonomous professional

Although the Labour Party was committed to comprehensivisation from 1942 onwards (Aldgate and Richards, 1999), and the 1944 Education Act allowed for multilateral schooling, the 'common' school did not make an impact until two decades later. In the 1960s the Labour government began to implement its policy of comprehensive education as part of the aim of achieving a truly egalitarian society – although the public school system remained unaffected by comprehensivisation.

Ironically, the move towards the comprehensive state system was in the hands of former public school boy, Anthony Crosland, a revolutionary Secretary of State for Education. Six months after taking office, the famous circular published by the Education Department, 10/65, 'requested' – not required – local education authorities to go comprehensive. Crosland had vowed: 'If it's the last thing I do I'm going to destroy every fucking grammar school in England. And Wales. And Northern Ireland' (cited by Timmins, 1995: 237). Unlike some more recent Secretaries of State for Education, Crosland recognised the status and autonomy of teachers' professional judgements and gave them the right to decide what was taught in schools: 'I didn't regard myself or my officials as in the slightest degree competent to interfere with the curriculum. We're educational politicians and administrators, not professional educationists' (cited by Francis, 2001: 14).

The recognition of status and autonomy is important: Hargreaves (2000) identifies this era in the 1970s as one of innovation in the teaching profession, when curriculum projects and individual teacher initiatives were encouraged. As members of the teaching profession were increasingly university graduates, they were more ready to involve themselves in educational debate. One debate was the concern among psychologists over the implications of eleven plus testing – the viability of selection based on the validity of a test. Coupled with sociologists' arguments about the role of environmental factors in affecting students' progress in school, there arose in educational circles what became known as the nature/nurture debate.

After the publication of Circular 10/65, the majority of local education authorities began to reorganise along comprehensive lines. In terms of autonomy, status and morale, the teaching profession had never had it so good: Penguin Education books flourished; teachers contributed to curriculum development via organisations such as the Schools Council; and teacher status reached new heights, supported by the substantial pay award of 1973 (Simon, 1991).

One of the comprehensive system's serious enemies was the media. As the print media continued to sing the praises of grammar schools, what in effect had become a bi-partite system of grammar and secondary modern schools remained untouched in a number of areas across the country. As Kerckhoff *et al* observe, 'At no time has there been a *fully selective* or a *fully comprehensive* system in England and Wales' (1996: 269).

Figures for 1970/71 show that the number of comprehensive schools stood at 1,313 with secondary modern schools close behind at 1,164, and grammar schools at 673 (adapted from *Social Trends* 2000). Thus the secondary modern school still provided the education with which most of the film audiences were familiar, so its portrayal did not disappear that quickly from the *reel* world of teaching. In 1971, the film *Please Sir!* was distributed, a spin off from the remarkably popular television series of the same name. It featured the naïve Bernard Hedges in his first job as a newly qualified teacher at the inner city Fenn Street secondary modern school. Here he is surrounded by a team of teachers who carry on in the *Carry On* style. Morris Cromwell is the well-meaning but ineffectual headteacher, supported by his formidable deputy head, Doris Ewell. Price is the science and maths teacher (heard to say that 'when Berlioz wrote *The March to the Scaffold* he was thinking of the first day of term at Fenn Street bloody school'), with Smithy, long past retirement, still teaching at Fenn Street. *Please Sir!* is a parody, 'the most palatable of critical approaches, offering insights through laughter' (Gehring 1988: 146). The *Morning Star* (Myers, 14/10/70) reinforced this point when it commented on the television series: 'it's far more satisfying to view the entire series as a dig at the crippling inadequacies of the State school system'.

Mr Hedges is given the daunting task of being the form tutor for 5C, whose nomenclature suggests that the students were in the bottom stream of the school (streaming grades students into ability categories and puts them in the same teaching group for all their subjects) and unlikely to be entered for public examinations. It was quite likely that the form tutor of the students at the bottom of the secondary modern school was also their main subject teacher for non-practical elements of the curriculum – a continuation of primary school ideology where one teacher has traditionally been largely responsible for almost all of the form's teaching. The closer relationship with a particular class was also in line with developments in pastoral care.

The film version of the television series goes beyond the confines of the classroom and shows Mr Hedges and his form taking part in the annual camp. Before this current academic year, 5C has never been allowed to go on a school trip. Thanks to Mr Hedges' appeal to the staff that his form are exactly the type of students to benefit from this type of extra-curricular activity – he is obviously a supporter of the fashionable cultural deprivation theory – they are permitted to go. Unusually, Doris Ewell sees his point of view and agrees the school might be shirking their responsibilities for these students who live in 'concrete canyons'. Mr Hedges must have the honour of accompanying them.

One of the students has a problem with getting written permission to go to camp from his parents, but this is quickly sorted out by his friends who trick the caretaker into signing his form. Once they arrive at the camp, 5C get into a series of scrapes, particularly with a 'posh' school that is sharing the facilities. However, once the students realise how Mr Hedges has supported them, they turn themselves around and begin to outstrip the other schools in various competitions.

Just when things are going well, the theft is discovered of £40 from the dormitory of another school. Along with the student at the camp without his parents' permission, the incidents lead the headteacher to declaim that the theft has 'put the mark of Cain on Fenn Street as a seat of learning' and that 'the lights are going out over Fenn Street'. However, on his arrival at the camp, both matters are happily resolved and the week ends with the ubiquitous party for staff and students.

Characterisation of the idealistic teacher in Bernard Hedges is at its peak in this film: 'If we only reach one child, our efforts will not have been in vain'. When 5C appear to respond enthusiastically to the outdoor life, not only does he praise them to the barmaid of the local pub to which he escapes on his night off, he also makes a reference to the major outlet of education journalism in the real world:

> I've been vindicated. Yes, it's fantastic. They're sweeping the board ... Do you know, only today in Environmental Studies ... Sorry, I'm sounding like the *Times Educational Supplement*.

Mr Hedges demonstrates the tutor's loyalty to the form. Whilst other teachers describe 5C as 'anarchic' – a description that other members of staff such as Mr Price, the token cynic of the staffroom, would adhere to – Mr Hedges sees them as being 'a little difficult' at times. Anarchy in schools, particularly comprehensives, was causing alarm in some circles. The controversy over comprehensive schooling reached a peak in the late 1970s, when some journalists in London who had children in inner city comprehensive schools reacted in print to the size of some of the schools and the lack of discipline. Jill Tweedle of the *Guardian* (09/12/74) reported: 'My eyeballs are gritty and swollen. My head rings like a gong. I am jumpy and irritable, my stomach curdles with indigestible emotions. I have spent the day in a large London comprehensive school.'

In 1977, *Panorama* produced a fly-on-the-wall documentary of Faraday High School in Ealing, showing unruly students and incompetent teachers. Despite controversy over how the programme was made and whether it was representative, it reinforced the worrying findings about the progressive teaching and learning styles at William Tyndale primary school revealed by a local education authority inspection. The current head of Ofsted, David Bell, recently attacked this era, describing the teaching in primary schools as 'plain crackers' (Smithers, *Guardian*, 06/10/04). Teachers claimed that it was their professional right to decide what was taught and how, as pertained in most schools at the time.

For parents, the type of schooling their children were receiving in both sectors of education bore little resemblance to what they themselves had experienced, but it is important to remember that the ethos underlying comprehensivisation was primarily social, not educational. But there was little evidence to show that this type of school would produce a classless, and therefore equal, society. The physical proximity of students of different backgrounds, interests and abilities did not ensure a better social mix. In reality, comprehensive schools used streaming as an internal selection device, which some educationalists saw as the tri-partite system under one roof.

As the number of comprehensive schools grew, Lowe (1997) cites geographical location as becoming the key variable: in the suburbs and in rural areas, comprehensive schools offered middle-class parents an acceptable alternative to a grammar school education for their children. But the inner city comprehensive schools could seldom be more than alternative secondary modern schools for students from lower socio-economic backgrounds.

Comprehensivisation was held responsible for the alleged decline in social discipline, general standards and basic skills. The effect of the William Tyndale affair spread to the teaching profession as a whole and inhibited teachers' ability to take part in educational debate (Dale, 1989). A moral panic about schools opened the door to the New Right to shape Conservative government's strategy. One election poster produced by Saatchi and Saatchi carried the strapline 'Educashun isn't working'.

In 1979 any teacher who was not already shell-shocked must have winced at the brute nihilism of the chart-topping single 'Another brick in the wall'. It was not a good time to be a teacher. (Timmins, 1995: 328)

When Margaret Thatcher became Prime Minister in 1979, with the Conservatives remaining in government for the next 18 years, another radical overhaul of the education system had begun. The stage was set to bring about change in the teaching profession: the media had played its part in influencing the Conservatives' views that schools were in chaos (Lawton, 1994). As Margaret Thatcher was the first Secretary of State for Education to become Prime Minister, it is not surprising that education came to the fore in the 1980s. The many innovations were made possible by the Conservatives' long spell in power:

The iron had entered [Margaret Thatcher's] soul as far as education was concerned during her time as Education Secretary. She had not forgotten the culture of the Department for Education and the education establishment which she had felt had been obstructive, patronising and complacent. (Baker, 2000b: 21)

The age of the collegial professional

Much to her chagrin, Margaret Thatcher's years at the department of Education and Science (1970-1974) had seen the continued comprehensivisation of the secondary school system. The initial effect of comprehensivisation on the teaching profession was to make bedfellows of teachers from two distinct teaching cultures. Both internal and external restructuring brought together those teachers who put subject expertise first – typically the university graduates and grammar school teachers – and those who favoured educational theory above subject knowledge – the college Certificate of Education, later BEd, holders and secondary modern school teachers. The belief that grammar schools were better than their secondary modern counterparts extended to promoting the more highly-qualified former grammar school teachers to the senior posts.

Although it was difficult to establish common ideological ground in the early days of comprehensivisation, with time – over 20 years – a collegiate and collaborative atmosphere developed as teachers increasingly turned away from government and towards each other for professional development and support. Faced with the implementation of numerous curriculum developments, the decline in professional status and the increasing 'social work' nature of the job, teachers collaborated on issues of gender and race via equal opportunity initiatives, and the inclusion of children with special educational needs into mainstream schools:

> The comprehensive school had a difficult birth. It was always an unwanted child for some, who impatiently awaited an opportunity to commit a discreet infanticide. For others it was an infant prodigy which needed to be carefully nurtured and to be defended against serious enemies. It survived. (Hargreaves, 1982: 161)

Thus by the mid-1980s there were many successful comprehensives up and down the country, such as Eltham Green. Its head was Peter Dawson, the inspiration for the character Brian Stimpson, the headteacher of Thomas Tomkin comprehensive school in the 1986 film *Clockwise*. Michael Frayn, writer of the screenplay, admitted that the main character bore 'more than a passing resemblance' to Peter Dawson (Sheldon, *Mail on Sunday*, 30/03/86). In the film Brian Stimpson copies Peter Dawson, using binoculars and the Tannoy system to survey and surprise miscreants in the playground (Staples, 31/08/87).

Thomas Tompkin is a successful, if somewhat obscure, suburban comprehensive school. As its headteacher, Brian Stimpson has become one of a select number of state school members of the prestigious Headmasters' Conference schools drawn from the private school sector, and is to address its annual meeting as its new chairman. On the day of the conference, he tells his students at Assembly:

> Today, today I take over as Chairman, Chairman of the Headmasters' Conference, and I shall be the first Chair in the whole history – in the whole of history – who is headmaster of an ordinary, common-all-garden, state comprehensive school, so it really is one for the Guinness Book of Records.

When he misses the train for Norwich, he seeks some other way to get to the meeting on time. He gradually goes to pieces as he struggles to complete his eventful journey in the company of a schoolgirl whom he has persuaded to take him to Norwich in her parents' car (despite his concern over her missing lessons) and a former girlfriend he was at training college with, who throws light on his murky past. The old

Brian Stimpson was always late, because the buses were on strike or he got the wrong train; he was even late collecting his diploma. Meanwhile, at the conference, there is concern that he hasn't arrived. Somehow, at 5.00 p.m. on the dot, Brian Stimpson arrives, somewhat the worse for wear from his troublesome journey – and is taken into police custody.

The satirical and scholastic edge to the film is particularly prominent in Stimpson's cutting comments on student attitudes – all too familiar to real world teachers – which are made 'public' as he continues to mentally rehearse his speech, from which he has become separated, on his way to the meeting:

> Does the sun ever appear late over the horizon saying, 'Please Sir, the bus was full, the train was on strike...'
>
> Does the tide ever go out during a study period saying, 'Please Sir, I'm having a row with my boyfriend ...'

And at the climax of the film, when Brian Stimpson finally makes it to the Headmasters' Conference, begins his speech and is continually interrupted by latecomers, he observes:

> I'm beginning to wonder if I'd be the only person in the world who would be slightly surprised if the tide came wandering in half an hour after the lesson had started, slammed all the doors, and stood there gazing round the room, trying to find some chums to sit next to while the rest of us patiently waited to get on with the day's events ...

Two years after the release of *Clockwise* came the other seminal Education Act of the twentieth century, the 1988 (Baker) Act. This was to prove to be only the tip of the iceberg when it came to educational reform. Teachers' level of professional autonomy was weakened by the introduction of a national curriculum. The perceptions of employers from industry and commerce that general standards and basic skills were declining were listened to, while teachers' professional opinions, channelled through their unions, were ignored: members of both teacher samples have experienced this. The public's perception of the teacher unions significantly contributed to the demonisation of the teaching profession, and the Conservatives took advantage of the media's anti-union stance (Regan and Regan, 1996). By the 1990s, the teacher unions had lost their power, in common with all unions; their role is now minimal, as education policy has been removed from public debate (Avis, 1991).

The 1988 Education Reform Act heralded a plethora of initiatives throughout the 1990s. When a policy did not deliver, it was succeeded by another before it had been in place long enough for its effect to be evaluated. The resultant policy landscape and its underlying educational ideology was scarcely recognisable to teachers whose careers had begun in an era when there was such professional freedom. Just as wider society had developed a consumer culture, so education was not exempt from having its focus moved from the providers of a service to its customers.

The discourse foisted on to the real world of education was that of industry and commerce: its language became littered with terms such as client, curriculum delivery, customer, manager, quality assurance, product, and so on. Teachers found themselves operating within a regulated curriculum in a competitive school market, where the policy landscape pushed schooling in the direction of the corporate and industrial sector. Education was thus commodified because it could be measured, packaged and delivered, within a postmodern society in which consumer culture reigned.

The age of the post-professional or postmodern professional

Only a brief account can be provided here of what is an extremely complex phenomenon. The postmodern condition, 'a period which began in earnest somewhere around the 1970s (Hargreaves, 2000: 167), marked a profound economic, political and cultural transformation. Whilst teaching is not the only profession which has faced upheaval because of changes to these discourses which underpin society, teachers are prime casualties because of the work they do, economically because of the reduction of public spending via the Welfare State where a customer-oriented ethos has replaced one of public service, and politically because of the decline in widespread commitment to public above private good, now that competition has replaced cooperation in a post-welfare society. As Lortie (1975:102) points out, teaching has traditionally not been about rates of pay and speed of promotion, and individuals who do dwell on financial and professional advancement are treated with suspicion: 'The service ideal has extolled the virtue of giving more than one receives; the model teacher has been 'dedicated''.'

Hargreaves' (2000) fourth age may be seen as reprofessionalisation, whereby teaching has been revised to operate in a different way, in the sense that the profession is altering (but not necessarily improving). The cultural transformation of wider society has put emphasis on the playful input of mass media and popular culture as alternative sites of education. This contradicts the practical process of educating students, grounded within the discourse of modernity. Theoretically, however, the position of postmodernity as celebrating a plurality and fluidity of identities may encourage teachers to reject government imperatives on how to teach. According to Parker (1997: 152), the diversity encouraged by postmodernity 'flies in the face of current trends towards universality in curricula, teaching methods and assessment systems'.

Ignoring what teachers know – which has intensified through the four stages of professional development outlined here – brings the profession to a point where teachers feel that their working conditions and core values have not been taken into consideration. This places them in the position of compromising their own deeply-held beliefs about teaching.

Carlyle and Woods (2002) suggest that the reforms in education of the late 1980s and 1990s superimposed a new social identity on teachers which was at odds with their existing ideas of what it meant to be a teacher. Surely the reform which caused the greatest impact was the creation of Ofsted, whose remit is to improve standards of achievement and the quality of education, using registered independent inspectors who publicly report on the strengths and weaknesses of schools. Baker (1994) and Dunford (1998) identified the move as yet another development in the Ofgas, Ofwat and Oftel genre. In their evaluation of the effect of the Ofsted process on teachers, Woods and Jeffrey (1998) identify the complete takeover of teachers' professional and personal lives by the process – before and during the inspection week.

Staff at a Dorset comprehensive school made their feelings about the process of inspection clear: in protest against the system of grading teachers, they burnt the inspectors' assessments (Worsley, *Times Educational Supplement*, 22/05/98). Another teacher railed against the system thus:

> Ofsted is an instrument few of us deserve. If Mary Chipperfied had done to her animals what is done to teachers during Ofsted, there would be public outcry. (Devrell, *Independent Education*, 06/05/99)

Until November 2, 2000, the Machiavellian figure of Chris Woodhead, former Chief Inspector of Schools, was at the centre of the relationship between Ofsted and teachers. Woodhead was not reticent when it came to talking about the controversial work of Ofsted, so he was a gift for the media. Francis (2001: 73) points to the telling contrast between the leaders of the teaching unions who 'however intelligent and responsible, come across as dull' and Chris Woodhead, 'the lean, lone hero, prepared to speak his mind'.

After the departure of Woodhead, a damage limitation exercise was conducted by his successor, Mike Tomlinson, himself no slouch at pronouncing negative soundbites on the teaching profession. As head of the inspection team which brought the Ridings School to its knees in the mid-1990s, he said that discipline at the school was the worst he had ever witnessed (Garner, *Independent Education*, 25/04/02), and was quoted as saying, 'I do not give a monkey's toss for the teachers' (Carvel, *Guardian*, 05/02/97). However, by 2002, in just over a year in post as Chief Inspector, he left with a 'glowing report' (Revell, *Times Educational Supplement*, 01/03/02). Since May 2002, his successor, David Bell, continues within an ideology where the inspection process is still perceived as being done to teachers rather than with them.

In 2003, a new approach was outlined, which promised a lighter touch inspection. Visits would be shorter, and there would be an emphasis on self-evaluation so that teachers would have more involvement in assessing their own strengths and weaknesses. So from September 2005, although inspections will take place every three years rather than the current four to six, they will not last as long – two days rather than a week. The amount of notice of an inspection will also be cut, from six to 10 weeks' notice to between two and five working days, and in certain circumstances there will be no warning at all.

* * *

Eccentric charismatic teachers are embedded within comedy films, a genre which has been particularly popular in Britain. Comedies have mirrored changes in the history of the education system, such as the reorganisation of secondary schooling post second world war. Not only do such popular cultural documents provide entertainment, they also provide humorous social commentary and criticism of ways of working in institutions (Landy, 1991: Street, 1997). These films focus on teachers both at the chalkface and at management level.

In *It's Great To Be Young*, Mr Dingle wins his students over by sheer personality. His behaviour challenges the conformity of an ossified senior management team and this threatens his future at the school. His students play a crucial part in determining that future when they organise a sustained programme of protests to have him reinstated. Likewise, in *Carry On Teacher*, the students mastermind a campaign which will prevent their headteacher, Mr Wakefield, from gaining promotion and moving to another school. Although Bernard Hedges of *Please Sir!* has managed to curb the everyday excesses of his students and gained their grudging respect, there is a definite sense that he is walking a tightrope from which he might topple at any moment. In much the same way, the headteacher in *Clockwise*, Brian Stimpson, has worked hard to make his school one of the most successful comprehensives in the country, but it only takes one incident dramatically to undo all he has accomplished.

Mourby (2002) highlights the contrast between the real and *reel* worlds of teaching in his comments on *Please Sir!* He observes that 'teaching was much easier in the 1960s. There was room for eccentricity, even if it did mean that characters like Smithy could get away with sitting in the staffroom all day because he was too addled to teach' (*Times Educational Supplement*, 11/01/02).

Likewise, members of the teaching profession have moved on a parallel track from a pre-professional stage – Mr Dingle, and Mr Wakefield and his staff – through the age of the autonomous professional – Mr Hedges – and on to the collegial stage of professional development – Brian Stimpson. While British comedy films have arguably made light of the classroom realities teachers face, screen culture retains an important role in mapping a generation of professional change, an era which is familiar to members of the first teacher sample, but is now long gone in a post-professional or postmodern professional era. The story continues in the next chapter by mapping the televisual output from screen culture against on-going government reform.

Chapter 2

After *Clockwise*, British films ceased to feature teachers as the main character, so in order to continue the exploration of teacher representations in screen culture this chapter turns to the *reel* world of television. It examines three drama series, the first of which, *Hearts and Minds* (1995), was broadcast towards the end of eighteen years of Conservative government. The New Labour government took its first step in its modernisation of the teaching profession by restructuring pay. Mid-way through its first term, *Hope and Glory* (1999) was broadcast. In New Labour's second term it began remodelling the teaching workforce via the workload agreement. *Teachers* (2001 onwards) brings the British contribution to screen culture representations of the teaching profession up to date.

Hearts and Minds

The drama series *Hearts and Minds*, written by Jimmy McGovern, featured Drew McKenzie (played by Christopher Eccleston), a potential entrant to the teaching profession. McGovern, a former factory worker turned teacher, created a character who relived his own experiences. A former colleague of McGovern's had watched his growing disillusionment and claimed that Drew McKenzie was based on the writer's own experiences (McGavin, *Times Educational Supplement*, 03/03/95). McGovern's experience as a teacher from 1979 to 1983 left a deep impression on him. It also made him want to write a school-based drama; he alleged that *Hearts and Minds* was his most challenging project to date (Williams, *Times Educational Supplement*, 10/02/95). Set in a Liverpool comprehensive, the series is about an idealistic teacher-in-training who was formerly a shop steward in a factory but goes into teaching thinking he can make a difference.

The classic storyline of new teacher on the block meets lacklustre old timer is reinforced in Drew's first lesson with his mentor, Mr Shotton, who is droning on at the front of the class about a former poet laureate. The camera pans round the classroom, showing students who appear to be asleep or listening to a walkman, or passing notes. Drew is standing at the back of the classroom, watching the bored reactions of the students. When he is finally called on to take part in the lesson, he looks up. But Mr Shotton continues to drone on about poetry and the iambic pentameter, whilst the students doodle and play with scraps of paper. The scene then cuts to Drew teaching, walking round the classroom, reciting the poem, Cargoes, clicking his fingers in time to the rhythm he is stressing verbally. His mentor stops writing in a book and looks up worriedly. Slowly the students, all bar one, begin to join in, banging out the rhythm on the desks with their hands, and Mr Shotton is aghast at the class's response. Drew is clearly enjoying himself as he moves round the classroom, pumping his arms, repeating the words of the poem, with the students emphasising its rhythm even more strongly. Drew finishes triumphantly: 'This is rhythm, right? Rhythm and language ... poetry!' The bell goes, the students depart, Mr Shotton locks the door and moves off down the corridor with Drew, asking him why he would want to come to a school like this: nobody in their right mind would do a teaching practice here. Drew replies that he wants to work with disadvantaged kids.

Hearts and Minds was well received by the critics and inevitably comparisons were made with *reel* life counterparts from the film world. According to the *Independent 2* (Pearson, 19/02/95), the series was the real thing 'compared to the romantic fantasies of *To Sir With Love* [sic] and *Dead Poets Society*'. The *Mail on Sunday* (Viner, 19/02/95) went further: 'The scene in which Drew thumped out John Masefield's poem Cargoes on his pupils' desks made Robin Williams in *Dead Poets Society* look lethargic'. What was more, *Hearts and Minds* provided the audience with an opportunity to look into 'the fug of failure' of the staffroom (Pearson, *Independent 2*, 19/02/95).

But as the series develops, and as the marking piles up on the breakfast and bedside tables, Drew's family life begins to suffer. His wife has already had to put up with four years of training, and now in his probationary year Drew's mind is elsewhere when he is at home and he is still knackered after a day at school. Drew knows all too well how teaching takes its toll; if you do the job properly, you end up killing yourself, so why even try? Even he resorts to the flick and tick approach to marking books.

In school, matters go from bad to worse, with both students and staff. He catches some students thieving; a girl in his English group tries to commit suicide in the girls' toilets; and a black colleague accuses him of racism. In best charismatic teacher mode, he berates colleagues in the staffroom as bone idle and accuses them of feeding the students worksheets which frees one colleague to sit on her arse and knit in her spare time. He says they could bore for England.

There is also friction about the grant maintained status of the school. Teachers may remember the tensions created between the schools who remained within the local education authority's jurisdiction and those who opted out. Whilst Drew appears to favour opting out, many of his colleagues who have more experience of teaching do not. Yet supporting the headteacher over grant maintained status does not gain Drew any favours. After his probationary year, he is not offered a full time job. The headteacher decides that Drew is good but not exceptional. He has made mistakes in his first year of teaching, so it would be better to learn from these and start with a clean state and a wonderful reference elsewhere.

But before Drew goes, there is one last favour he can do for the headteacher. A visit from the inspectors has resulted in the end of Mr Shotton's career. Once as good a teacher as Drew, his energy has ebbed away over the years, the highs have got fewer, and teaching has settled into a long, safe, boring, job. Due to Mr Shotton's imminent departure, the school play is in need of a producer, and it is through this vehicle that Drew is able to wreak his revenge. What starts off as a tame production of *Julius Caesar* becomes a musical version updated for the twentieth century, with the plot subverted to show the headteacher up for what he truly is. With the audience firmly on Drew's side, the headteacher walks out.

But it is a hollow victory for Drew. Despite the suicidal girl coming on side for him and not wanting him to leave, and the colleague who accused him of racism congratulating him on the message behind the school play, Drew has had enough of teaching, and we see him in his back garden, burning his books on educational theory.

The first term of the New Labour government

Two years later, after eighteen years of negative Conservative government soundbites about incompetent teachers and failing schools, the
change of government in May 1997 was seen by many teachers as the
opportunity for positive change. Despite New Labour's election
promise of 'education, education, education', little was done to res-
tore teacher morale. In many ways, the education policies of New
Labour had much in common with the New Right reforms of the
1980s and early 1990s (Phillips, 2001): they would 'not change the
balance between pressure and support, as Tony Blair promised before
the 1997 general election' (Chitty and Dunford, 1999: 153). Even Chris
Woodhead was kept on as Chief Inspector of Schools at Ofsted.

In its first term of office New Labour continued to endorse education
ministers as the people to decide what should be taught in schools,
and to support a discourse which was centred on 'good' and 'bad'
teachers. According to Francis (2001: 41), David Blunkett, the Secretary of State for Education and Employment during New Labour's first
term, 'promised a new department style, seeking to unite, build a con-
sensus and rally all the talent and experience within our country and
elsewhere'. This did not happen: the disparaging of the profession,
which started under the Conservatives, continued to undermine
teacher status and morale, resulting in a crisis of retention and
recruitment.

Research reported in the *Guardian* (Elliott, 13/03/99) identified
teachers as the unhappiest group of public sector workers. Voluntary
Service Overseas had received an increase in applications from
teachers, who felt they could achieve more abroad than in contemporary Britain: 'A lot of teachers contacting us say they feel demoralised in their current jobs and want to go somewhere they will be
valued more highly. The public perception of teaching is poor'
(Carvel, *Guardian*, 25/02/99).

In a report for the National Union of Teachers, Alan Smithers and
Pamela Robinson claimed that nearly a third of all secondary school
teachers-in-training and a quarter of their primary school counterparts did not go into teaching after completing their courses: 'As one
trainee teacher who decided not to pursue it said to me, 'I thought
that I would meet loads of creative Dead Poets' Society [sic] people

but I just met people who were really into tick-boxes" (Fitzsimmons, *Guardian Education*, 09/01/01).

This reference to the influence of the *reel* world of teaching on aspirant teachers in the real world was reinforced by Gemma Warren, a regular columnist for the *Times Educational Supplement*. An important platform where real teachers can voice their side of things is the *Times Educational Supplement*, dubbed 'The Teachers' Paper'. It commands a unique position in the print media because it has a special agenda to incorporate the interests of both teachers *and* the media. After a year in teaching, Gemma Warren reflected: 'It didn't take me long to realise that, surprisingly enough, teaching is not like the movies. They don't show Michelle Pfeiffer up all night struggling to finish her marking' (*Times Educational Supplement*, 05/05/00).

In 1998, an anonymous article entitled *Dear Mr Blunkett* was singled out by the editor, Caroline St John-Brooks (30/11/98) as striking a chord with many members of the teaching profession, and it subsequently received prominent display on many school staffroom noticeboards. The writer of the article reflected:

> I see people who are exhausted, who are insulted daily by the children in their care, and who know that they are not valued by anyone very much. I've tried, really tried, because I felt that teaching was a mission to help others but at the end of the day – teaching is just a bloody awful job. (*Times Educational Supplement*, 06/11/98)

A departing teacher spoke for many of the escapees who were granted early retirement before the government was forced to change the criteria in 1997:

> I should be at the top of my profession. Not as a chief inspector, professor or headmaster, but simply as a teacher. I should be a real expert by now, informed, and organised, with my socio-psychological insights sharp and clear. I should be in my classroom delivering the goods. But I'm not, and nor are thousands like me. As soon as we could, in my case at 50, we left teaching, vowing never to go back. Has it occurred to anybody that something might be wrong? (Smith, *Times Educational Supplement*, 13/11/98)

One month later, an important publication of New Labour's first term in office was published: the Department for Education and Employment's consultative Green Paper. *Teachers: Meeting the Challenge of*

Change set out the case for modernising the teaching profession: 'We all need good teachers, whose skills and dedication are recognised and respected. That means a first class profession, well-led and well supported. It means backing high standards with high rewards, which recognise the talents of those who teach our children' (Summary:1). It would mean teachers embracing a professionalism which could respond swiftly and effectively to the social and educational changes arising from a postmodern society, and would result in the most fundamental changes experienced by teachers in the last one hundred years. The first stage of this modernisation would be about pay restructuring, and would be the major reform of New Labour's first term of government.

Because in postmodern society money talks louder than service and status, the idea of teaching as a vocation rewarded by societal respect has been replaced by being just a job with the emphasis on pay. The introduction of a dual track professional development system linked to performance related pay came as a shock to the teachers who had been in the profession a long time, the implication being that ability would now take precedence over commitment.

Francis (2001) observed that the print and broadcast media supported the performance related pay move: 'Every step of the way editorials were saying that this was common sense, that teachers were misguided to resist this move, that the government should hold its nerve and press ahead' (p32). An example of such support came from the *Guardian* (22/04/00): 'What is fair about a dedicated and exceptionally gifted teacher receiving the same pay – or even less if the teacher is young – than a clapped-out, clock-watching, uncreative time-server?'

The scheme had the potential to create a profession with two distinctly different cultural backgrounds, just as when grammar and secondary modern school teachers found themselves in the newly-created comprehensive system over 30 years ago. Introducing performance related pay was based on false assumptions of what motivates most teachers and drives them in their work. It was an extrinsic motivator, one that had little history of being a priority for teachers (Fullan and Hargreaves, 1992). Performance related pay might have relevance in the world of business and industry where it was possible to control the outcomes, but for teaching it was impractical (Crace, *Guardian Jobs and Money*, 08/05/99), as teaching does not produce visible and quantifiable results.

When the proposals for performance related pay were outlined in the 1998 Green Paper, it appeared that the majority of the 41,000 people who read the document were opposed to it. A national opinion poll for the National Association of Schoolmasters/Union of Women Teachers found that 45 per cent of teachers thought the proposals unfair, with only 17 per cent of those eligible willing to apply (Carvel, *Guardian*, 13/10/99). However, when the general secretary of the National Union of Teachers said that guidance for members applying to cross the threshold would be available from his union, performance related pay got the unofficial go-ahead from teachers (Carvel, *Guardian*, 18/02/00).

Applying to cross the threshold raised questions in the minds of members of the teaching profession at all levels and across all sectors of education: teachers voiced their concerns about eligibility to cross the threshold, and how teaching performance could be measured. A headteacher asked:

> How do I choose between the excellent and enthusiastic teacher of art, music and dance, the teacher who gives all to history and geography projects or the one who crams her class to get good test results. (Barnes, *Times Educational Supplement*, 02/04/99)

But eligibility was not the only issue; applying to cross the threshold also raised the issue of maintaining integrity. Applying meant going against an individual's beliefs, but not to apply meant risking one's career; subsequent success would engender feelings of guilt, but lack of success would lower morale (McManus, *Times Educational Supplement*, 02/06/00). Another contributor put the issue more crudely: 'So get real and apply. Or become an Untouchable and never work again' (Whitwham, *TES Friday*, 09/06/00).

Reports of opposition from members of the teaching profession proved unfounded. When the process got underway, it was estimated that 80 per cent of the 250,000 teachers eligible to cross the threshold to the upper pay spine applied in the first year (Dean *et al*, *Times Educational Supplement*, 16/06/00) and 97 per cent were successful. Opposition continued to crumble: according to a study of 95 teachers by Wragg, six out of ten who refused to apply in the first round did so in the second, and of 86 who failed, a third successfully appealed (Mansell *et al*, *Times Educational Supplement*, 14/12/01).

Five years later, the scheme continues to evolve. It has been announced that levels four and five of the upper pay spine are to be scrapped so that level three is now the ceiling for 80 per cent of the teaching profession, a lower level of pay than that proposed in 1998. This is not surprising: the move from level two to level three in 2004-2005 is causing enough financial headaches for schools (Stewart, *Times Educational Supplement*, 20/08/04). Levels four and five are to be replaced by an Excellent Teachers' scheme. There is also the complete overhaul of management allowances, to be replaced by Teaching and Learning Responsibility payments at two levels.

Removal of the automatic move to the next point on the main pay spine which those new to the profession join means that all teachers are now subject to performance related pay (Stewart, *Times Educational Supplement*, 19/03/04). Other pay issues include offering more money to teachers in subject shortage areas, and for working in certain geographical areas (Smithers, *Guardian Education*, 20/09/04). However, the same article claims that improved pay is not helping retention. As Grayling (*Guardian Saturday Review*, 01/09/01) reflects:

> When people lose sight of the invisible rewards on offer in different avocations and look only at that which provides the largest net balance at the bank, many kinds of work that make the world a better place suffer a loss of talent.

Hope and Glory

But it was a different government initiative about teachers which was the focus for the last television series in the twentieth century about teachers. *Hope and Glory* depicted a heroic new breed of school manager in the *reel* world of education – the superhead – brought in to save a failing (inner city) school and giving it a fresh start. The superhead followed on the heels of the 'superteacher' policy introduced in September 1998, whereby 'good' teachers (Advanced Skills Teachers) would be 'financially promoted' without leaving the classroom (Sutton *et al*, 2000).

Once again, comparisons with flashing blue light cops 'n docs series were inevitable: the makers of *Hope and Glory* claimed that they were creating a series on a par with *Casualty* (Brown, *Times Educational Supplement*, 09/04/99). The first series, with its inspiring storyline of superhead Ian George's sacrifice of a government post in favour of saving Hope Park School from closure, received positive responses from real world teachers (Buss, *TES Friday*, 23/06/00). Controller of BBC1 Peter Salmon claimed that *Hope and Glory* was the BBC's attempt to 'own' education, and in the light of the latest BBC Annual Report's warning that the channel's dramatic output was ignoring its public service broadcasting responsibilities, *Hope and Glory* received a peak time viewing slot (*Broadcast*, July 9, 1999). It demonstrated that teaching could provide as rich a source of drama as the police and hospital series, a proposal not lost on real world teachers (Buss, *TES Friday*, 23/06/00). In her book *Ahead of the Class* Marie Stubbs, who took over at St George's School, the inner city comprehensive in London where headteacher Philip Lawrence had been shot dead, refers to a piece in the *Times Educational Supplement* by Mike Baker 'in which he contrasts my 'old-fashioned' approach with that of Lenny Henry's laid-back headmaster in the series *Hope and Glory*' (Stubbs, 2003: p152).

In the opening episode of *Hope and Glory*, the storyline is again on the lines of out with the old – departing headteacher Neil Bruce – and in with the new – incoming superhead Ian George. The whole school is gathered in the hall with the male deputy headteacher, the head-teacher and some governors on the platform. A tatty banner bearing a farewell message is strung behind them. Two students whisper to one another: they have obviously set something up in order to disrupt the proceedings. At the back of the hall, Ian George enters via the swing doors, and moves to stand by one of the woman teachers; not the best of times to pop into his new school. Back on the platform, the headteacher receives his leaving gift, an electronic organiser and, after muted applause, begins his speech.

He does not get far before the sound of muttering begins. He and other members of staff round the hall try to quieten the students. Gradually, the students become louder; they are chanting the head-teacher's favourite slogan, 'end of story'. When he realises, he agrees with them – it is 'end of story' – a happy ending for both of them, he hopes. He tries to keep going as they get louder. He says, 'Come on now, that's enough, end of story ...', but by now the students are gesticulating, and when he shouts at them to stop, they take no notice. Finally, he focuses on one of the ringleaders and calls her a 'filthy little whore'. Immediately, the chanting stops. Students, staff and governors are horrified at this insult. But the headteacher has lost the plot: not only does he abuse the students – 'pigs', 'cretins', 'useless braindead morons', 'jail fodder', 'gutter snipes', 'dole cheats' – he takes himself and his colleagues to task for staying there to teach them. His life's work ...

According to the *Guardian* (Sweeting, 23/06/99):

> *Hope and Glory* has a strong cast, and [Lenny] Henry is surprisingly plausible, but would the high-flying Ian George really have turned down a prestigious and highly paid job as head of the government's new education task force, choosing to run the derelict Hope Park instead? Would the embittered retiring headteacher, Neil Bruce (Peter Davison), really have flayed his pupils with abuse at his leaving ceremony?

Writing in the *Times Educational Supplement* (09/07/99), Ted Wragg was likewise cautious: 'Lenny Henry's television enactment of the superhead who rescues a failing school ... is well acted and the hero is cheering, but duff schools need more than the odd half-hour turn round. The course is for stayers, not sprinters.' The writer of *Hope and Glory*, Lucy Gannon, was equally uncompromising in her point of view: 'Teaching is like nursing, or driving an ambulance – if you're not doing the job properly you're wrecking lives and you should get out' (Dodd, *Radio Times*, 19-25 June, 1999).

Once Ian George officially takes over, one of his first tasks is to appoint a woman as permanent deputy head, which causes the expected annoyance amongst the potential candidates. Obviously happy with his choice, he does not get on well with the deputy head he has inherited, and this feeling is reinforced when the latter is left in charge of the school for a day and a serious accident occurs. At the beginning of the final episode of the first series, Ian George takes assembly. The surroundings have become opulent and intimate, indicated by the purple curtains and majestic music. Ian George is in that unenviable position of announcing the arrival of Ofsted inspectors. With his staff gathered on the stage behind him in a position of moral support, he has just made the assembled students laugh. They fall silent as he continues: 'I mean it ... I will. I'll go and meet those inspectors at the front gate tomorrow morning and I'll say, 'Come in ... come in and welcome!' because they are. I want them to come in and see everything, I want the whole world to come in and see everything, because I'm proud of this school – of the staff and of each and every one of you. Her Majesty's Inspectors? I'd be happy if it was Her Majesty herself, but if she can't make it then her inspectors will just have to do.'

The visit of the inspectors leaves Ian George saddled with a permanent watchdog from the local education authority on his tail. Things begin to fall apart as his senior management team disintegrates: he commits professional suicide by sleeping with his woman deputy head, and has yet more run-ins with the other deputy head. Thus, the upbeat ending to the first series turns to downbeat by the end of the second.

Hope and Glory generated articles in the print media from members of the real world teaching profession about their *reel* world counterparts. In a letter to the *Radio Times* (November 25 – December 1, 2000), Jeff Hartley hoped that the *reel* world of teaching might affect government policy. He praised Lucy Gannon for 'having the courage to show how the barrage of Government initiatives, accountability, Ofsted inspections and unremitting drive towards 'raising standards' and improving GCSE and SAT results have driven teachers over the edge':

> If this one programme makes the Government and public sit up and think about teachers' conditions of work, it will have done an enormous service towards lessening the enormous pressure under which they work.

By the start of the third series, two new deputy heads are in place, and Ian George has sorted out his personal life. But problems continue to escalate, so much so that Hope Park will be put on special measures should it fail after the return visit of the inspectors. Just when things cannot get any worse, a rooftop siege involving a suicidal member of staff ends in tragedy. When attempting to talk the teacher away from the edge of the roof, Ian George suffers a heart attack.

The second term of the New Labour government

The general election of June 2001 saw a new Secretary of State for the newly-named Department for Education and Skills, Estelle Morris. A former teacher at a city comprehensive school, she became a Member of Parliament in 1992 (Woodward, *Guardian Education,* 12/06/01). Together with David Blunkett, she helped modernise the teaching profession. He dealt with pay and she with conditions, beginning the process which led to the workload contract of September 2003. She wanted to change the existing contract which contained an open-ended clause, worded to indicate that teachers were expected to do any additional tasks required to fulfil their professional duties. In January 2002, she started to identify a list of tasks teachers should not be expected to do, but before the official start of the workload agreement, she became an early – and unexpected – casualty of New Labour education policy and resigned in October 2002 after only 16 months in post. Estelle Morris was good at dealing with the teaching profession – she realised that the government's attacks on teachers were self-defeating, and that what was needed was to have them on their side (Judd, *Report,* January 2004) – but she was not as good at dealing with the media (Wintour and Watt, *Guardian,* 24/10/02).

In the last 30 plus years, Education Secretaries have stayed in post for about two-and-a-half-years on average (Hill, *Report,* March 2004). Estelle Morris's successor, the fourteenth Secretary of State since 1973 was, according to the National Union of Teachers' Secretary, worse than any holder of the post during Margaret Thatcher's reign of terror (Smithers, *Guardian Education,* 08/04/03). A *Times Educational Supplement* survey of 500 primary and secondary teachers (Passmore, 19-26 December, 2003) showed that only 47 per cent knew that his name was Charles Clarke.

The workload agreement, which came into effect from September 2003 and which was agreed on by all the teaching unions bar the National Union of Teachers, meant that teachers could refuse to carry out 24 administrative tasks. The largest teaching union did not sign the workload agreement because of the issue of assistants replacing teachers in some situations (Revell, *Guardian,* 23/10/02). But would using assistants be preferable to redeployed civil servants (Stewart and Shaw, *Times Educational Supplement,* 20/02/04), or members of the Women's Institute (Lee, *Times Educational Supplement,* 19/11/04)?

Over time, teachers will increasingly be released from tasks they have performed for many years. From September 2004, cover for absent colleagues was restricted to an average of one hour a week. From September 2005, teachers will no longer invigilate exams, and time must be given for planning, preparation and assessment. Such moves are intended to improve the work/life balance, and it is true that bulk photocopying and taking minutes at meetings are activities which few teachers miss doing. However, activities such as putting up classroom displays or phoning a parent to investigate student absence underpin the role of teacher and tutor and should not be put into other hands. Furthermore, teachers have traditionally not asked people to do things they were not prepared to do themselves (Richards, *Church Times*, 11/06/04) so it comes hard to treat non-teaching staff as minions rather than colleagues. On the other hand, perhaps the removal of 'menial', manual tasks will allow the profession to leave behind its union roots and attain the professional status it has craved for so long?

As well as the start of the workload agreement, Clarke's other significant influence on school policies was to suggest extending the school day from 8.00 a.m. to 6.00 p.m. in order to provide childcare for the parents. But after two years in post, he was moved to the Home Office, and in December 2004, Ruth Kelly, the youngest female cabinet member ever, took over. As she has been a journalist, she should know how to handle the media.

Teachers

Despite Francis's (2001: 241) plea for 'intelligent, adult versions of school and teachers and television drama', Channel 4's *Teachers* (2001 onwards) does not appear to be so. According to Mark Lawson: 'In common with the heroes of all adult school dramas on television or in cinema, Simon [Casey] is an inspirational maverick who wins the respect of the students by breaking the rules' (*G2*, 19/03/01). Writing in the *Times Educational Supplement* (16/04/01), Ted Wragg was enraged by the first episode of the series, labelling the central character as a 'monumental prat ... Within the first episode he had managed to do several things that would have had a real teacher up on a disciplinary charge.' Wragg declares that: 'the ultimately convincing drama about teaching is yet to be written'.

According to producer Jane Fallon, the main aim was to make an 'entertaining, light and approachable show' (Howard, *Time Out*, March 21-28, 2001). This approach was reinforced by Andrew Lincoln who played the main character Simon Casey, when he described the series as a 'weird and exciting but – most importantly – fictional world' (http://www.channel4.com/talk/pastchat, 29/04/01). But maybe the 'negative' stereotypes of *Teachers* would 'counter-intuitively do what teaching dramas have so far failed to do, and finally succeed in getting the real-life teachers' message across' (Orr, *Independent Review*, 20/03/01). One teacher wrote in to the *Times Educational Supplement*'s website that the series 'shows people who are the opposite of boring middle aged schoolmarms with perms, obsessed with poor pay and mounting paperwork' (http://www.tes. co.uk/have_your_say ..., 26/03/01).

In the first series, Simon and his colleagues Brian, Kurt, Susan and Jenny work in the somewhat surreal environment of Summerdown School, a Bristol comprehensive. Simon's first appearance begins with a prank – breaking into Summerdown School on the evening of his birthday, depositing a sheep in a laboratory, and stealing a bust of Shakespeare as a souvenir – and this sets the tone for the level of professionalism.

The first series managed to pack in many aspects of school life familiar to real world teachers: Parents' Evening, the Open Day for prospective year 7 students, leaving day for year 11, the (embarrassing) personal and social education lesson on sexual intercourse, and Simon having to apply for the job he has been doing because it was initially a temporary post. *Teachers* came under fire from the Professional Association of Teachers at their annual conference for portraying teachers as 'heavy drinking, lazy, dishonest and irresponsible', and thereby bringing the profession into disrepute (Smithers, *Guardian*, 03/08/01). The union passed a motion underlining the importance of teachers acting as positive role models to counteract the negative image of the profession in screen culture. MacQueen (*Big Issue*, 11-17 March 2002) responded to this: 'real teachers are the most humourless profession on the planet, and always complain about anything that presents them as less than saintly'. When the *Guardian* asked a group of teachers to watch the first two episodes of *Teachers*, some of the audience fell asleep: 'While the Summerdown teachers seem to think nothing of going out and getting trashed every night of the week, our real ones are in a state of semi-permanent knackeredness' (Crace, *Guardian Education*, 27/03/01).

In the second series, it became increasingly harder to identify links to the real world: 'If *Teachers* were a pupil you would give it 100 lines to write after school' (Joseph, *The Times*, 14/03/02). New staff joined Summerdown School, Penny, a newly qualified teacher who struggled to get a grip on the job, and JP, who stood up to the headteacher's demands for extra duties. Again, aspects of school life familiar to real world teachers featured – a careers fair, a drive on pastoral care via an Open Door policy, a talk on teenage pregnancy from an ex-student, a stationery amnesty, an end of term staff party – but more as a back-drop to the personal lives of the teachers. It was during the second series that Simon left.

Series three had Matt established in Simon's place, Lindsay also joined the staff, and Susan, Jenny and JP left. *Teachers* continued to run storylines about getting laid and/or getting drunk. Increased focus on the personal lives of the main characters left little room for school issues, although romance between colleagues, becoming acting Head of Department and thereby alienating your former friends, boys' underachievement and taking on new initiatives such as acting as stress partners are all familiar in real world schools. The political incorrectness of Brian and Kurt was demonstrated by their actions during Mental Health Week: Kurt put someone in detention for 'being a mong', and Brian called someone a 'spastic' on the foot-ball pitch. Their behaviour during exam invigilation was childish in the extreme, both rushing over to a student desk with more paper and hoping to arrive first, but any teacher who has done exam invigilation will know just how tedious it can be. Teaching continued to be por-trayed as 'an inconvenience to be squeezed into a tight timetable of gossiping and boozing' (*The Guide*, 9-15 August, 2003). And yet *Teachers* is popular, because of its 'engagingly shoddy circle of Friends Behaving Badly – who just happen to be teachers' (Ford, *Big Issue*, August 4-10, 2003).

One episode from the third series merits special attention. Lindsay is criticised as a poor role model by the menopausal headteacher who issues her with a verbal warning. This causes her to take stock, and to confide in Bob. Ironically, he suggests she take a look at some films about teachers to get some inspiration. He rattles off a list of his favourites: *Goodbye, Mr. Chips, Blackboard Jungle, Dangerous Minds* ('an urban classic'), *The Prime of Miss Jean Brodie, To Sir, With Love, Dead Poets Society* ... This leads to her mimicking John Keating *et al*, and she withdraws from her circle of friends both physically – she stops drinking and going to the pub – and mentally – she enjoys school and all its attendant activities. Ironically, when Lindsay is enthusiastic about teaching, she is regarded as strange, and her friends begin to dump their problem students on her as she seems to have the answers. Bob likewise experiences a renaissance in his teaching when he emulates John Keating, much to the derision of his students.

Needless to say, Lindsay is unable to keep up her new approach to teaching – starting a lunchtime Biology club to liberate frogs, turning the football pitch into a nature reserve, making the place where the teachers smoke into a peace garden. The post-menopausal head-teacher comes to her senses and berates Lindsay for wasting time on out-of-class activities which encourage students to be free spirits. Lindsay goes in search of Bob and finds a bottle of whisky in his office: normal service is resumed.

Teachers is the first Channel 4 drama to be commissioned for a fourth series, making it the channel's most successful drama ever (Crossley, G2, 26/10/04). 'Alternative career-enhancement tips' continue to be on offer to real world teachers (Bloom, *Times Educational Supplement*, 25/06/04). None of the original cast remain. Brian, Kurt and Matt are no more; in the first episode of series four we see their graves being urinated on by their former colleagues. New staff have arrived: Ben, an atheist, who teaches Religious Education; Damien, who teaches Food Technology; and Ewan, the Head of English. Funnily enough, they behave exactly like the deceased trio did.

These new teachers are from Wattkins Comprehensive School, which the former inmates of Summerdown School have been forced to join, due to its closure. As Ewan is Head of English, Bob has been demoted, and is now behaving extraordinarily badly. Weekly themes reinforce the political incorrectness of these professionals: religious tolerance; obesity awareness; gay and lesbian awareness; race awareness are all flouted. The school secretary becomes the chair of the Parent Teacher Association, and wields her new-found power by blackmailing the teachers to write positive reports about her wayward daughter. Penny sleeps with a student. As Lindsay points out, somewhat strongly, a teacher/student sexual relationship is the worst thing you can do, other than run amock with a gun. Every episode ends in chaos in the pub, and the student incidents which are so obviously ignored by the staff become ever more surreal.

Jane Fallon believes that the 'cringeworthy classroom moments' explain the series' appeal in real world staffrooms: the events which happen are grounded in reality, but because they are situated in the *reel* world they always go pear-shaped (Bloom, *Times Educational Supplement*, 25/06/04). If you can get past the swearing, the smoking, the laddish obsessions with all matters sexual, these *reel* world teachers are free to say the things real world teachers are often thinking.

An episode when an Ofsted inspector calls merits a special mention. The teachers trash the school at the end of term party and the registered inspector turns up the next day. The headteacher is expecting a man, and reminds the female staff to go for the maxim 'skirt and flirt'. When they see that it's a woman, she has to be locked up in the headteacher's office whilst Plan B is put into action. With the dinner ladies manning an operations room, an imported class of unimpeachable students are moved from teacher to teacher while the usual students are put out of sight in a mobile classroom. When they are discovered crucifying Ben, Ewan is drafted in to flirt with the inspector in order to save the school. Can this bunch of *reel* world teachers really survive the inspection and move into a fifth series?

* * *

The fictional television teachers mirror their film counterparts by featuring the charismatic teacher who makes a difference. Drew McKenzie of *Hearts and Minds* has left his previous employment and is on a one-man rescue mission to save the most disaffected of students, but what started as enthusiasm and commitment ends in disillusionment. *Hope and Glory*'s Ian George is a charismatic teacher who has passed up the opportunity of a high-flying government post to rescue yet another group of dispirited students – this time, a whole school full of them – but the stress of the job catches up with him and his heart condition. In both *Hearts and Minds* and *Hope and Glory*, the new teacher on the block is contrasted with the old. Polly Toynbee highlights the importance of these texts for real world teaching when she writes 'an even better enticement into the profession than more pay, golden hellos or advertising comes from gripping television dramas and documentaries that turn teachers into heroes and heroines' (*Radio Times*, 17-23 March, 2001).

However, Simon Casey in *Teachers* heralds a change in the portrayal of the charismatic teacher. He is not an altruistic or idealistic hero: he is, in the words of Mike Baker (*Times Educational Supplement*, 11/05/01), 'an amoral, selfish young man whose conscience has been surgically removed'. But Baker observes that real world teachers are sympathetic to Simon 'because they would like to see themselves as free-wheeling, uncaring individuals'. The series succeeds because of the way that 'the on-screen teachers break the rules so gloriously' (Diary, *Times Educational Supplement*, 15/08/03). What members of the second teacher sample thought about the Channel 4 series *Teachers* is revealed in chapter six.

Chapter 3

This chapter focuses on the life course of the teacher as portrayed in the enduring charismatic teacher film. The nature and degree of commitment to teaching varies with individual life stages, and Sikes *et al*'s (1985) and Woods' (1995) accounts of the development of the teaching life cycle show how a teacher's career and professional development are placed within the wider context of their life outside school. The teaching life cycle also provides a generalised outline of a career throughout its duration.

The *reel* world of the enduring charismatic teacher has its roots in the biographical film and offers a longitudinal view of the life and times of a teacher's career. Like *Blackboard Jungle, Goodbye, Mr. Chips* (1939) is another yardstick for the charismatic teacher film. James Hilton, the writer of the film screenplay, wrote a letter to Robert Donat, the actor who won an Oscar for his portrayal of the legendary *reel* teacher, in which he said:

> The old schoolmaster has also been pictured so many times, by book and magazine illustrators, and in so many different styles, that I have come to the conclusion that there must indeed be many Mr Chips in existence. (Trewin, 1968:105)

According to Warburton (1998) Mr Chips has become a nickname for teachers. 'It has been used in many contexts subsequently as a figure of speech representing the traditional 'caring' values of teachers' (p254). *Mr Holland's Opus* (1995) is an updated version of *Goodbye, Mr. Chips* for the 1990s. Like Mr Chipping's charges, 'Mr Holland's students are resolutely average – they are neither ghetto kids waiting to be saved, nor would-be geniuses waiting to bloom'.

Don't worry if you're overworked, underpaid, and unappreciated, your reward lies in all those young minds you've opened to higher things. Teachers, however flattered, may feel Stephen Herek's movie takes a rather sanitised view of classroom life. In 30 years at the chalkface, Glenn Holland encounters an amazingly clean and well-behaved succession of kids. (Kemp, *Sight and Sound,* May 1996: 56)

In the real world, those 30 years begin with training to be a teacher. Exploring the teacher life cycle therefore starts with entry into the teaching profession.

'No one Forgets a Good Teacher'

The 1944 Education Act was not the only government policy to impinge on the development of the teaching profession at that time. The McNair Report, published in the same year, dealt specifically with the training of teachers and called for teaching to become an academic profession, with teachers-in-training to be given some knowledge of the philosophical bases of teaching and education, rather than only trained in practical competences. Up to the beginning of the 1960s the most usual route taken into teaching was the two-year certificate of education offered by teacher training colleges.

The change in the education system from tri-partite to comprehensive in the early 1960s was similarly mirrored in training institutions, with the majority of potential entrants to the teaching profession being trained for longer in colleges of education. Bell (cited by Alexander, 1984) has identified the change of nomenclature as symbolic of the shift in ethos regarding the balance between academic theory and practical training. It was during the early 1960s that the proposal first arose of making teacher training a degree course and creating the 'subject' of education as a university discipline (Wilkin, 1996). The development of the Bachelor of Education degree (BEd) should have given the teaching profession higher status in society, bringing it into line with law and medicine. However, amongst those critical of such training were teachers already out in schools, who felt that the existing theoretical input provided by training institutions got in the way of the real practical experience of how to cope in the classroom (Wilkin, 1996).

By the early 1980s, teaching had become an all-graduate profession, and although the four year BEd course provided time for the study of education, the thirty-six week Postgraduate Certificate of Education (PGCE) course became the major route into teaching in both primary and secondary schools, which implies that the decision to teach is made later than immediately after finishing school. Just as schools were part of the political backwater before 1979, so the training of teachers as a policy area was left to the academics in higher education until the early 1980s. Circular 3/84 underpinned the establishment of the Council for the Accreditation of Teacher Education to 'manage' higher education, and under Circular 24/89 the Articled and Licensed Teacher schemes became additional routes into teaching which put the emphasis on school experience. The creation of the Teacher Training Agency in 1994 resulted in even more external control. In the creation of a national curriculum for teacher educators (Hartley, 1998), aspirant teachers must show themselves competent against a long list of statements. Critics of this approach, such as Trend (1997), argue that the process of teaching cannot be reduced in this way: it prevents the development of creative teachers.

It seems that the Teacher Training Agency will bend over backwards to find a way into the profession for would-be teachers, in the belief that the proliferation of routes is one way of tackling the teacher recruitment problem. Persuading men and women of university age to become teachers is a serious concern for the government: in a climate in which public services do not have the appeal they had for graduates in pre-Thatcherite days; people fresh out of university can make far more money in business and industry (Else, *Times Educational Supplement*, 03/08/01). Thus, along with the diversity of routes has had to come the introduction of financial incentives: a training salary for postgraduates, golden hellos for those training in shortage subjects, and a fast track programme for high fliers. Alongside the BEd and PGCE courses is School Centred Initial Teacher Training, run by consortia of local schools. The certificates they offer have parity of esteem with those awarded by higher education institutions. On-the-job salaried training is offered via the Graduate Training Programme or the Registered Training Programme.

But according to Calderhead and Shorrock (1997), the role of intrinsic motivation must not be underestimated as the reason people enter the teaching profession and enjoy their work; governments need to realise the importance of quality of work to teachers (Fullan and Hargreaves, 1992). Utilising another aspect of screen culture, advertising has enabled the government to proclaim the non-financial incentives of becoming a teacher.

Advertising to persuade people into the teaching profession is not a new idea in Britain; it was used during the last major period of teacher shortages after the second world war. Between 1944 and 1951, 35,000 ex-servicemen and women were trained under emergency schemes, some of just three months duration (Aldrich, 1996). Fifty years on, in September 1997, the government and the Teacher Training Agency began an advertising campaign in cinemas and on television. Dyer (1982) asserts that the most successful television commercials are those which feature actors, sports personalities and other celebrities. Accordingly, well-known people led a ten million pound campaign to try and prevent an impending shortage of teachers and raise their status, by naming their favourite teacher under the slogan 'No one Forgets a Good Teacher'.

Seventeen celebrities appear in a variety of situations. Some are just head and shoulders shots: Jeremy Paxman, Joanna Lumley, Skunk Anasie, Bob Hoskins. Some are situated at home in surroundings which suggest how successful they have been: Ben Elton, David Seaman, Eddie Izzard. Others are posed beside props or artefacts which remind the viewer of how they made their name: Terence Conran appears in front of a Habitat-style set of shelving which is laden with Habitat-style china; Lord Puttnam stands before a (film) screen; Bruce Oldfield poses in front of pages of fashion designs; Stephen Hawking sits in front of a blackboard full of mathematical notes. Yet others are pictured with props/artefacts, which demonstrate a key interest in their lives, by which they are also known: Anita Roddick stands before a board which proclaims 'Because We're Women'; John Cleese appears in a garden accompanied by animals. Some celebrities are pictured in the workplace: Michael Grade appears in an office; Sebastian Coe is outside the Houses of Parliament; Tony Blair sits at his desk in Number 10; Steve McManaman kicks a ball around at his local rec. The importance of teachers in the lives of students is emphasised in two ways: each celebrity looks straight to camera and says the name of the teacher who influenced them, and the setting in which the celebrity is shown implies that they would not be where they are today had they not been inspired by that teacher. After the last of the seventeen celebrities, up comes the catchphrase 'No one Forgets a Good Teacher'.

People from the worlds of entertainment, sport, business and politics named their most influential teachers, with Tony Blair being the first serving Prime Minister to star in an advert (Judd, *Independent*, 15/10/97; O'Leary, *The Times*, 15/10/97). However, Ralph Tabberer, the chief executive of the Teacher Training Agency, announced that the ten million pound campaign had been a flop. He said that it had had no impact; in fact, numbers of students entering initial teacher training dropped by 16 per cent between 1996 and 1999 (Mansell *et al*, *Times Educational Supplement*, 02/06/00). It was left to an editorial in the *Times Educational Supplement* (22/04/00) to put its finger on the most successful innovation which would attract people into the teaching profession: 'Attracting those who grew up in the 'greed is good' culture was never going to be easy. Belatedly, the Government has gone for most graduates' soft spot – their wallets.'

Despite setbacks, the Teacher Training Agency persevered with their advertising initiative, and the 2000-2001 and 2001-2002 series were designed to be more subtle and challenging (Thornton, *Times Educational Supplement*, 27/10/00). These were underpinned by the message 'Those who can, teach', an inversion of G B Shaw's well-known dictum which has dogged the teaching profession for far too long.

The 2003 campaign introduced yet another slogan 'Use your head. Teach.' Images of headless workers in offices implied that there were more interesting jobs to be done elsewhere which would be of greater benefit to people seeking meaningful employment. The underlying message that being a teacher was in an individual's best interests was supported by David Hart, general secretary of the National Association of Headteachers: 'A poorly paid vocation without good career prospects and with a heavy workload is not going to be attractive' (Thornton and Pyke, *Times Educational Supplement*, 22/08/03).

These adverts caused some controversy, and were superseded by the latest campaign, in which working with children is the selling point (Paton, *Times Educational Supplement*, 03/09/04). 'Use your head. Teach.' now underpins images of laughing students, supported by straplines such as 'Work with the most exciting people in the country'. Whether it is the draw of promises that working with children is better than any anti-ageing cream, or the financial incentives on offer for training – or both – recruitment into the teaching profession is no longer the worry it was a decade ago.

Vocation in the *reel* world: early days

Because time can be collapsed in the *reel* world of film, insights are provided into the longitudinal careers of teachers as they progress through the teaching life cycle. In the real world, teachers experience a particular stage or stages of a colleague's career; they very rarely see the whole picture, the career in its totality. Fullan and Hargreaves (1992) voice the questions which those new to the profession might ask themselves when they encounter their older staffroom colleagues:

> Have you ever wondered what these 55 time servers were like when they were 35, or 25? Were they just ticking over then too? Were they that cynical? Is it possible that they were once as bright-eyed and idealistic as many of their younger colleagues are now? And if they were, what happened to them in the meantime? Why did they change? (p37)

Biographical film enables glimpses to be seen of the life and times of two enduring charismatic teachers, Mr Chipping and Mr Holland. Both are men 'looking back on a lifetime in front of the blackboard' (Buss, *Times Educational Supplement*, 24/05/96). *Goodbye, Mr. Chips,* distributed in 1939 and based on the book of the same name by James Hilton, was originally intended to be a vehicle for Charles Laughton and Myrna Loy, but was revised for Robert Donat and Greer Garson (Glancy, 1999). It is interesting to speculate whether the film would have become the touchstone it has, not only in the real world of teaching but also in the *reel* world, had it starred the originally intended actors.

The real world teaching life cycle states that at the birth of a career individuals are likely to be idealistic about it and to see it as a vocation (Sikes *et al*, 1985), and Mr Chipping is no exception. On his first day at Brookfield School, he is assigned to supervise lower school prep.

Mr Chipping enters the suspiciously silent classroom; the students regard him angelically. Then his mortar board is pulled from his head, and what appeared to be a quiet room full of smartly-uniformed, innocent-looking boys quickly turns into bedlam. One of the ring-leaders has got hold of the mortar board and, offering to clean it, deliberately makes matters worse by rubbing chalk into it from the blackboard duster. Mr Chipping finally gets the students back to their places, and sets the homework; he offers to answer any questions they might have about the set task. Nervously he sits down, checking the seat for more traps.

The students look prepared for more mischief. Taking him at his word, one starts by asking an irrelevant question, and then the rest join in, trying to trap Mr Chipping into giving embarrassing answers. Whatever he does compounds the damage already done. Silence is finally regained, then another question is asked, over the spelling of the word 'Armada'. The whole class joins in, shouting out possible spellings, and the scene descends into bedlam once again.

This time, the headteacher arrives and restores order. The students clear to reveal Mr Chipping in disarray. He apologises to the head-teacher: 'I'm afraid I ...' ('lost control'?) The headteacher will punish the boys, and also wants to see Mr Chipping in his study later on.

At this interview, the importance of exercising authority and the dif-ficulties of teaching are reinforced. Young men such as Mr Chipping might find other careers better suited to this stage in their life: it takes more than a university degree to be a good teacher. Mr Chipping is devastated, and hopes he will not be asked to resign on the spot as it has meant everything to him to come to the school. He grits his teeth when the headteacher reminds Mr Chipping that it will take courage to face the students again. The headteacher can forget the incident, but can the boys? If Mr Chipping is willing to carry on, the head-teacher will watch his progress with interest. As he leaves the head-teacher's study, Mr Chipping encounters two colleagues who have heard about the debacle and tells them that the boys will not humiliate him again.

Another film which provides a longitudinal study of a teacher's career is *Mr Holland's Opus*, made over 50 years later in 1995. It begins in a state school in the 1960s. Mr Holland differs significantly from Mr

Chipping in that teaching is his second choice of career: he is first and foremost a musician. Indeed, Mr Holland informs the principal, Mrs Jacobs, that he got his teaching certificate as something to fall back on – not the most auspicious of beginnings! It is obvious that, unlike Mr Chipping, teaching is not initially a vocation for Mr Holland – and he is not alone: in the real world, research has shown that the eventual decision to enter the profession is often last resort rather than first choice.

> One teacher, reflecting on her immediate contemporaries in a one-year postgraduate training course, claimed that of fifteen would-be secondary science teachers only one had always wanted to be a teacher, adding that if, as a graduate, you hadn't a job 'teaching was something you fell into'. (Jenkins, *Times Educational Supplement*, 07/11/97)

Furthermore, the perception of teaching as a vocation was a 'myth'. According to Jim Donnelly from Leeds University: 'I think teaching has always been the kind of occupation that people go into if their circumstances require it' (Edwards, *Times Educational Supplement*, 19/11/99). There were more pressing reasons for going into teaching, financial circumstances being one of them. Unlike medicine and the law, the decision to enter teaching can be deferred until late in an undergraduate course or, once a graduate, taken at almost any stage of adult life, and Mr Holland's circumstances do require him to take that step!

Sitting in the school canteen with one of his new colleagues, Bill Meister, the PE teacher, Glenn Holland explains what he has been do-ing with his time up until now – ten years on the road as a musician – and why he would rather teach music in a school than play it in night clubs. He believes he will get free time for composing, because he is first and foremost a composer. Bill Meister laughs at him and ques-tions Glenn Holland's reasoning over the time issue, as he cannot remember when he last had free time. Glenn Holland looks aghast at this information.

When he arrives home, his wife attempts to cheer him up with the money she has made with her photography that day: thirty-two dollars. Glenn Holland responds that he made thirty-two kids sleep with their eyes open. He is beginning to realise just what a rough gig he has let himself in for; when he was a student, it never occurred to him that his teachers might want to be somewhere else rather than the classroom.

Time passes, and a few months into the job, Mr Holland is approached by the principal and asked to join an after-school committee. When he responds that he does not have the time, Mrs Jacobs informs him that she has been watching him since he came to the school, how he rushes for the parking lot at the end of the school day. When he protests that he is doing his job, she informs him that teachers have two jobs, to fill young minds with knowledge, but also to provide those young minds with a direction to go in. She does not know what he is doing with the knowledge, but on providing a direction as a compass he is stuck.

This conversation appears to reinforce his hatred of teaching, but as his wife is now pregnant, there is no way he can give up the job, so he must seek an alternative approach to make his life in school easier. After some routine questioning of the class at the beginning of his next lesson, he admits to them that he has not had any impact on them in the last few months. He asks them to be honest when he asks them what kind of music they like and they all admit to rock'n'roll, apart from the class creep, of course. Mr Holland sits down at the piano and plays some popular music – after all, he has been a studio musician. When he asks them questions about it, they respond far more readily. At the sound of rock'n'roll coming from Mr Holland's classroom, the deputy principal, Gene Wolters, arrives to investigate. At home that evening Glenn Holland enthuses to his wife about how much fun his day was.

The greater the performance – the greater the distance between the teaching persona and who the person really is – the greater the strain teaching will be on the individual (Lindley, 1993). Mr Holland is stuck: in his personal life, because he cannot give up his day job and also, according to the watchful eye of the principal, in his professional life. He has to do something to change: once the reluctant new music teacher and anxious to get back to his real work of composition, as time passes he re-channels his passion for music into his students. He starts off a disciplinarian, but comes to realise that he gets better results when he synthesises the classical with the contemporary and begins to close the gap between his teaching persona and who he really is, and to experience the intrinsic rewards of teaching: 'he is a music lover who uses what the kids naturally like as a teaching tool so that they will take notice and see a teacher experimenting with different methods – something usually not found in movies' (Chumo II, *Films in Review*, May-June, 1996: 63).

In the real world, the rewards on offer for the charismatic teacher are also extrinsic.

'And the winner is ...'

Teaching 'Oscars' were first awarded in 1999. As the innovator of the Teaching Awards Scheme and first chair of the General Teaching Council, Lord Puttnam is regarded as a genuine champion of the teaching profession (Wilson, *Teachers*, July 2001) who will take on the media over its negative presentation of teachers.

The re-emphasising of teaching as a profession, a status-enhancing and morale-boosting strategy, was implicit in the creation of the General Teaching Council for England (GTC). There had been attempts for over 150 years to establish a self-regulatory body for the profession (compared with the creation of the General Teaching Council for Scotland in 1965). A key characteristic of professionalism is the existence of professional associations, and until September 2000 teachers were the only major profession in England and Wales without such a body, having chosen instead to form unions to represent their workforce in negotiating pay and conditions, although they are white-collar workers. Because the state took a major role in the provision of schooling ever since the Education Act of 1870, it was not in its interests to allow teachers the professional independence of the medical profession, who experienced no form of state interference until the National Health Service was introduced in 1947.

The first English General Teaching Council had 55 members, 66 per cent of whom had current experience of working in schools (Mansell and Dean, *Times Educational Supplement*, 07/07/00). Despite Lord Puttnam's obvious support for the teaching profession (appearing in the 'No one Forgets a Good Teacher' advert), his appointment and time as first Chair of the English GTC was dogged by controversy. In contrast, the first chief executive of the equivalent for Wales was a former history teacher, Gary Brace (*Times Educational Supplement*, 24/3/00). A letter to the *Times Educational Supplement* (Jones, 10/12/99) was not appreciative of Lord Puttnam's appointment, and reflected the ongoing resistance to intervention in teaching from those who were not real teachers: 'Presumably, on this logic, Ken Dodd will be pressurised to lead the BMA and Alex Ferguson will be evidently suited to chair the Law Society'.

There was an attempt by the National Union of Teachers to replace Lord Puttnam after his first year as chair of the GTC but he was unopposed (Mansell, *Times Educational Supplement*, 22/06/01; Smithers, *Guardian Education*, 03/07/01). At the same time as he was laying the foundation for the GTC, Lord Puttnam also took on the chair of the Teaching Awards Trust, established in 1998. This is a registered charity independent of government which relies on sponsorship from the world of business and industry. David Hart, general secretary of the National Association of Headteachers, is a trustee.

According to the latest information sent to schools (The Teaching Awards Trust, October 2004), the reasons for making an 'Oscar' nomination include publicly recognising the 'unsung heroes' in a school and the 'amazing work' they do in changing student lives: 'Teachers make a difference – make a difference to a teacher'. 'Oscars' are awarded in categories such as best new teacher, teacher of the year, and contribution to school leadership (all awarded to both primary and secondary school teachers), and there is also a lifetime achievement award. The awards process aims to highlight the benefits of choosing to join the teaching profession, and is supported not only by all political parties and teaching unions but also by the BBC, who demonstrate their commitment by broadcasting the annual awards evening.

However, the innovation initially received mixed reviews from the print media. Writing in *Guardian Education* before the first awards evening, one commentator observed:

> So if televised Oscar ceremonies help to put bums on cinema seats, it is more likely that when the satisfied customers in our schools appear on our screens each year, praising the work of teachers, then a grateful nation will sit up and take notice. It is certain that such ceremonies will have a more positive effect on public opinion than a ran-

corous NUT Easter conference or some sclerotic teacher union leader demonstrating just how out of touch with the real world he [sic] can be. (Mooney, 08/12/98)

Critics of the scheme felt that an Oscar ceremony was not an appropriate way to reward teachers: 'An Oscar might adorn the mantelpiece but you can't raise a mortgage on the strength of it and fobbing off teachers with glitzy evenings and statuettes is, well, tacky' (Moriarty, *Guardian*, 14/07/98).

The broadcast of the first awards evening at 7.00 p.m. on a Sunday on BBC1 began with upbeat music, with visuals of students and teachers overlaid with words in large lettering: 'stimulating, encouraging, challenging'. Moving into the studio, Gaby Roslin and Stephen Fry took their places as the presenters for the evening. She was the straight woman of the duo, sticking to the facts and figures – who won how much and for what: £500 (initial nomination), rising to £3,500 (regional winner) to £20,000 (national winner). He was the comic who made somewhat cynical comments – 'the physical manifestation of the nation's gratitude takes the form of a small perspex cylinder with a bearded man on it' – but tempered these with such accolades as calling teaching 'humanity's highest calling', for which he got a heartfelt round of applause. Stephen Fry told the audience that Plato 'didn't have to referee soccer matches twice a week, supervise the chess club, keep the keys to the computer room, mount a school play, schmooze with parents, stay up marking till two in the morning and put up with syllabus changes every fortnight. Plato had it easy ...' (cue for another round of applause). After this introduction, a minute's montage of school life was shown, again underpinned by 'inspiring' music: the playground, the classroom, the school crossing, pastoral care, field trips, experiments, games, school dinners. Maureen Lipman was the presenter of the first award, Best New Teacher in a Primary School. Stephen Fry remarked that new teachers are brave souls: even now as he remembers the first lesson he ever taught, his bowels begin to loosen. Before the award was made he invited the audience to look at some of the teacher's work. The videotape rolled ...

According to the *Independent* (Judd, 15/07/99):

Here were people who toil away out of the public eye featured on prime-time television because of their extraordinary skill in a profession which holds the key to children's futures. Lord Puttnam, who ran the awards, was surely right to argue that such public recognition will raise the status and morale of teachers – who have been under fire from politicians and the media for more than 20 years. ... Several of the winners were at pains to emphasise that there are plenty of teachers of similar calibre out there. 'I'm nothing special,' one said.

In an article in the *Times Educational Supplement* (09/07/99), Lord Puttnam quoted the Chief Rabbi, Dr Jonathan Sacks: 'We have lots of heroes today – sportsmen, media personalities, supermodels. They come, they have their fifteen minutes of fame and they go. But the influence of a good teacher stays with us. They are the people who really shape our life.' Lord Puttnam continued: 'But the fact of the matter is, it's all too easy to take the work of these exceptional individuals for granted.'

Since the first awards evening, the status of the event has altered, with changes of time, day and channel of broadcast, and presenters. The broadcast was relegated from the peak time Sunday schedule to the late afternoon snooze slot and then to a late night weekday slot, as well as changing channel. Gaby Roslin and Stephen Fry have been replaced by one presenter: Davina McCall of *Big Brother* in 2000, Carol Smillie of *Changing Rooms* in 2001 and 2002, and Eamonn Holmes from 2003 onwards. But the awards evening of 2004 went out on a Sunday evening at 7.00 p.m. on BBC2. As ongoing chair of the Teaching Awards Trust, Lord Puttnam (*Guardian Education*, 26/10/04) continues to champion the teaching profession:

> People often ask me to what extent the Teaching Awards reflect what is happening within the teaching profession. The good news is that, despite some early concerns, the awards have come to mirror the best of what is going on in education. Recruitment, and the uptake of professional development, continue to improve in both numbers and quality; just as nominations have increased five-fold since 1999. And, as chair of judges Ted Wragg confirms, our judges are of the opinion that the quality of nominations gets better year on year.

But what about the teachers who do not experience that fifteen minutes of fame? Faced with the problem that on average between one-quarter and one-third of those who enter the teaching profession leave after five years, returning to the *reel* world is useful in showing how Mr Chips and Mr Holland come to terms with staying on in the profession.

Vocation in the *reel* world: mid-career

Mr Chipping has failed to move on to another school (i.e. Harrow) and has not yet gained internal promotion to a more pastoral role as housemaster at Brookfield, because his strength is perceived to lie in his teaching and learning style in the classroom. In the real world, as Sikes *et al* (1985) point out, whilst teaching is seen as a worthwhile job, in mid-career its place in an individual's value-system can lose its initial significance; Francis (2001) suggest that middle-aged teachers can face a long period of work which affords them no new challenges. Mr Chipping experiences frustration until someone from outside the profession steps in and helps him see his career in a different light. The biographical film provides a window on to the private lives of teachers: on holiday in Austria with a colleague from Brookfield, Mr Chipping meets Katherine Ellis, who later becomes his wife.

Mr Chipping has gone climbing alone and is lost in a heavy mist. He hears a woman calling and thinking her in need of rescue, he makes the treacherous way towards where he thinks she is. When he finds her, they settle down to share his coat and her sandwiches, and strike up a conversation. When offered a penny for his thoughts, Mr Chipping admits that he has been reflecting on what his life as a teacher has caused him to miss out on, namely attractive and charming women like Katherine. Emboldened by her response that the women have missed out too, and the feeling of exhilaration caused by being lost on a mountain shrouded in mist, out of the world and out of time, he is emboldened to ask her whether she thinks a person of his age could start life over again and make a go of it.

Katherine: It must be tremendously interesting to be a schoolmaster.

Mr Chipping: I thought so once.

Katherine: To watch boys grow up and help them along, see their characters develop and what they become when they leave school and the world gets hold of them. I don't see how you could ever get old in a world that's always young. (And that is part of the problem: what Katherine fails to appreciate is that as teachers get older, their students remain the same age, which reinforces the ageing process for teachers.)

Mr Chipping: I never really though of it that way. When you talk about it you make it sound exciting and heroic.

Katherine: It is.

Mr Chipping has sensed that this is a make-or-break moment in his life, not only personally but also professionally. He wants to know whether he, a middle-aged, mid-career individual, has any hope for the future. Is he exciting and heroic too? She assures him that he is, and as if to reinforce the re-launching of his life and his career, the thick mist which had enveloped them on the mountain begins to clear. Back to reality, says Mr Chipping – but there is the sense that this will be a changed reality.

In the latter years of Mr Chipping's career, his wife enables the newly nicknamed Mr Chips to see his life and work in a new light which enables him to build a stronger sense of vocation at Brookfield. He begins to reach out to his students beyond the classroom, by inviting then to Sunday tea, and by visiting the wife and child of one of his ex-students. When boredom and cynicism could all too easily have taken hold, his enthusiasm is re-kindled.

What began for Mr Holland as cynicism and a lack of involvement has been transformed into enthusiasm for teaching. Offering a full range of extra-curricular activities, which all music teachers are accustomed to doing, he provides personal tuition and starts up a marching band. 'Mr Holland works to bring out the best in students who need his help in different ways: the shy clarinet player who needs to put more emotion into her music; the athlete who has to learn a musical instrument quickly' (Chumo II, *Films in Review*, May-June, 1996: 63).

Twenty years after he joined John F Kennedy High School at the start of his teaching career, Mr Holland is preparing to involve himself with yet another aspect of musical extra-curricular activity, the annual school production. The teachers are gathered for a staff meeting. The deputy principal, Gene Wolters, has been promoted to principal on the retirement of the former incumbent, and he is obviously a very different kettle of fish to Mrs Jacobs. She had appointed Mr Holland and after his inauspicious beginning he had become her favourite teacher. But the wider education climate has also changed. Although the proposed senior class play, a George and Ira Gershwin review in which Mr Holland would obviously have a major input, is relatively cheap to produce, it may still have to be cut due to shortage of funds.

This creates some uproar, but Mr Holland's close friend and colleague, Bill Meister, comes up with an idea which will guarantee the school production makes a profit: he will teach the football players to dance, and this will bring the punters in. With the help of Mr Holland, he strikes an appropriate pose to illustrate his claim. Levity wins the day, and the auditions go ahead. The underlying financial implications make this production even more important. Mr Holland becomes so absorbed in writing the musical arrangements that he misses a Science Fair evening for parents at his son's school. When Mrs Holland and his excited son Cole return from the evening at school, Mr Holland is slaving away at the piano.

Mrs Holland: I thought you were going to meet us.

Mr Holland: Well, I wanted to, but I had to get these orchestrations finished by the end of the week for the kids. We're going to do a Gershwin review.

Mrs Holland: It's always something, isn't it? If it isn't a school play, it's band practice, or grading papers, or some student committee needs an advisor. ... Why is every other child more important to you than your child?

Mr Holland: I'm a teacher, Iris.

Mrs Holland: You are his father.

Mr Holland: I'm both. I do one thing, I let him down. I do another thing, I let the school down. ... I do the best I goddamn can, OK?

Mrs Holland: Well you know what? Your best isn't good enough. So, go on, write your music.

Mr Holland: Write my music? Write my music? When do I get time to write my music?

This conflict with his home life is a scenario familiar to real world teachers. But teaching has traditionally appealed to altruism and idealism in the individual, and both Mr Chips and Mr Holland are teachers whose approach to their work is underpinned by these characteristics. Perhaps the times both men are portrayed working in supported the notion of a job for life, and in the case of the teaching profession this was 40 years of service to education. Do these *reel* world counterparts therefore belong to an old way of teaching which is no longer viable in what we have identified as a postmodern age?

Vocation in the real world

In the modern age, Lortie (1975) argued that teachers saw their work as service, with a traditional emphasis on what he calls 'psychic rewards' (p101). More recently, Grayling still supported this view of teaching: 'For vocation it is: no one who has chosen teaching over some other occupation on merely pragmatic grounds has been able to stick it, unless they fell in love with it' (*Guardian Saturday Review*, 01/09/01).

In the past, teaching was often linked with medicine and the law, as each performs an essential public service, entry to each involves a lengthy period of initial education and training to master theoretical knowledge and practical skills, and each is complemented by continuing professional growth. However, as a vocation, teaching has arguably more in common with the ministry (Lindley, 1993; McManus, 1996), because the qualities required by a teacher are more closely bound to creating successful personal relationships than demonstrating technical craft, whereas lawyers and medics are encouraged to maintain a distance from the clients they serve (Goodson, cited by Hargreaves and Lo, 2000). Weinstein (1998: 242) reinforces the link between teaching and the ministry by reference to the *reel* world: 'In the cinema of schooling, the cause is education. School is its church, the means through which the task of redemption be accomplished, and teachers are its evangelists.'

Teachers may question the notion of teaching as a vocation which is implicit in these films and they are not alone. In the minutes taken during the Education and Employment committee (Education) Sub-Committee on February 9, 2000, Lord Puttnam goes further: 'We are also quite wrong in thinking that there was a golden era of Mr Chips in which everything was wonderful' (p6). However, Goodlad (1990) stipulates that 'ignoring the appeal of teaching as a calling is a serious error' (p15).

Whilst the chief executive of the Teacher Training Agency, Ralph Tabberer, acknowledges the value of having people in the profession who regard teaching as a 40 year career, he also realises that:

> We might be better getting five to ten years' worth of energy and experience out of people and then replacing them with other professionals who have proved themselves in industry or in other professions. (Tester, *Report*, March 2000)

It may be that that calling now comes later in a person's life: 'With the money-obsessed 80s and 90s behind us, and popular series such as Channel 4's *Teachers* helping the profession shed its stuffy image, a record 40,000 people began training to be teachers this year' (Asthana and Townsend, *Observer*, 11/04/04). So teaching has become *the* job to have – probably the most popular career change – as individuals swap the boardroom and office politics for the classroom. The number of people beginning teacher training schemes is 50 per cent greater than it was in 2000. Teaching 'can provide a mid-life redemption' (Jeffries, *G2*, 18/02/04) and this is reinforced by reports in the print media of former government special advisor, Jo Moore – who sent *that* e-mail on the day of the terrorist attack on the United States – and former chief speech writer, Peter Hyman – who coined *that* 1997 New Labour election slogan – taking up posts as a classroom assistant and a teaching assistant respectively in schools in north London. For people joining the profession in the twenty first century, often after having had experience of other workplaces, becoming a teacher is perhaps an opportunity to give something back to society.

Vocation in the *reel* world: latter days

In his seminal work, Waller (1932) identifies the toll teaching can take on the individual. The constant demand to discipline and punish erodes optimism, and the immature minds of the students drag the teacher's mature mind down – 'one cannot see the man for the school master' (p382). Teaching is thus more advantageous to the students than it is to the teacher; traditionally there has been an emphasis on societal benefit, a public service ideal, rather than on personal gain.

Whilst Fullan and Hargreaves (1992) suggest that disillusionment and disappointment are inevitable as teachers age, Sikes *et al* (1985) and Woods (1995) point to the importance of teachers' mid-careers as the defining factor underpinning the harvest of the teaching life cycle, resulting in feelings of either stability or stagnation. Commitment to the profession becomes more instrumental: material reward gains in importance and teaching takes a more peripheral place in teachers' lives. The latter stage of the teaching life cycle is a time of decline in physical energy which puts enthusiasm to the test (Fullan and Hargreaves, 1992).

In the *reel* world, enthusiasm lives on. As he nears the end of his teaching career, Mr Chips is asked to see the new headteacher of Brookfield. Dr Ralston is already seated behind his desk when Mr Chips is called in. The headteacher is keen for Mr Chips to consider retiring. When Mr Chips responds that he does not want to, the headteacher explains that Mr Chips is out of date in the direction he wishes to take the school, for example, with regard to his teaching and learning styles in Latin. He also comments on his physical appearance, which is shabby. Mr Chips takes the new headteacher to task: he regrets the passing of old ways and witnessing the school becoming an institution where all that matters is a fat bank account. The ethos of Brookfield has changed, the boys who should be there cannot afford to be and the school is being run like a factory: presaging Thatcherite ideology! He is not going to retire.

Word of their disagreement spreads amongst the student body, who are aghast that Mr Chips should be asked to retire. He taught their fathers: if he went, the whole place would fall down. One student even threatens to kill the headteacher. Mr Chips also has the support of his teaching colleagues and the governing body. He recognises that compromise is called for, as the school has need of both him and the new headteacher.

Five years on, Dr Ralston publicly admits his mistake in having asked Mr Chips to retire when he did. Now that the day has finally come, no one regrets more than he that Mr Chips will be retiring. There is tumultuous applause as one of the students presents him with a retirement gift, for which all subscribed willingly. Mr Chips has become a much-loved teacher – enduring but also endearing.

'Battered by his first class at Brookfield, Charles Edward Chipping sticks it out' (Trewin, 1968: 105). Having retired at 65 after teaching for 43 years at Brookfield, Mr Chips is asked to become acting headteacher during the years 1914-1918, taking his final tally to a remarkable 48 years. Mr Chips' services are needed by the governors who wish him to be headteacher, as no-one living knows the school as he does. When the current headteacher remarks on his lonely life and says it is a pity he never had any children, Mr Chips responds that he has had 'thousands of them, thousands of them, and all boys!' By the time of his death, Mr Chips has spent 63 years at the school.

As a late entrant to the profession, Mr Holland manages 30 years before being made redundant, or 'taking retirement'. Compare this with the real world, where the number of teachers aged 60 and over in the profession fell by 53 per cent between 1990 and 2000, with less than 1 per cent of the profession over 60 (Howson, *Times Educational Supplement*, 09/11/01).

Mr Holland's exit from the profession does not start out as such a happy one. He appears not to have much to say in the matter of his 'retirement'; cuts in education are required, as he already knows from his experience with the school production, and now he is one of them. Thirty years on from when he entered the teaching profession, Mr Holland wakes up and wonders what happened to his life.

Bill Meister and Glenn Holland are in the latter's teaching room on what appears to be his last day at the school. When asked what he is going to do with this time, Glenn Holland responds that he is too old to start a rock band, and that he is not retiring but getting dumped. His friend has nothing to worry about: the day they cut the football budget will be the end of western civilisation as they know it. He is scared, and he does not think he will be missed. He was dragged into this gig, kicking and screaming, and now teaching is the only thing he wants to do. He has given his whole life – he has worked for 30 years – because he thought what he did made a difference, that he mattered to people. However, he has discovered that he is expendable. Bill Meister leaves him sitting at his piano.

The scene cuts to the hall and the very first student whom Mr Holland helped when she was having such difficulty over playing the clarinet is making a speech about his retirement. The hall is packed, testimony to the effect of Mr Holland's teaching career. The speaker says that Mr Holland has had a profound influence on everyone present. When she was at school, there was a rumour that Mr Holland was writing a symphony which would make him rich and famous. This had not happened. He has not misspent his time, nor is he a failure. Indeed he had achieved a success far beyond riches and fame. There was not a person there whose life had not been touched by him. Each one of us, she claims, is a better person because of Mr Holland: 'We are the music of his life.' Thus Mr Holland experiences the same recognition as Mr Chips.

True to the sentimentality inherent in the genre, the Everyman schoolteacher is celebrated in the end as a hero, and he learns his true 'opus' is not the one he struggled to write for years but rather the lives he has touched and helped form. Holland's triumph may bring tears to the eyes, but there is nonetheless an underlying truth about it. We get the sense that Mr Holland transformed lives one-by-one throughout the years, often in the smallest of ways. (Chumo II, *Films in Review*, May-June 1996: 63)

Once again, the charismatic teacher film encourages those in the real world to hold on to those elements of their work which feed intrinsic motivation. Mr Holland's last lesson is to appreciate his own worth – but is that enough? In the way it devours the self and takes over one's life, teaching is not an ordinary job.

* * *

The lives and times of Mr Chips and Mr Holland provide a longitudinal picture of a teacher's career and a more individual approach to professional change and development than that described in the previous two chapters. Two men dedicate their lives to their work: for them, teaching is a vocation. Mr Chips had always wanted to be a teacher, whilst Mr Holland had started life as a studio musician. The effect of their dedication on their personal and professional lives means that Mr Chips finds love late in life, but his happiness is cut short when his wife dies in childbirth, and he has to learn to soldier on without her. Mr Holland has to learn to balance family life with his teaching commitments throughout his professional career. What is their reward for their unremitting devotion to duty? Whilst Mr Chips decides to retire, Mr Holland faces redundancy.

As in the case of the eccentric charismatic teacher film, the enduring charismatic teacher film also maps a way of teaching which is fast disappearing in the creation of what Furlong (2001:129) and McCulloch (2001:103) have termed a 'new professionalism'. If 'culture carries the community's historically generated and collectively shared solutions to its new and inexperienced membership' (Hargreaves, 1996: 320), it is important that those coming into the profession recognise their historical antecedents and the process of professional change and development which charismatic teacher films provide.

Chapter 4

This chapter traces 50 years of charismatic teacher films. The focus for each is the first encounter of teacher and students, as this provides insight into how to – or more often how not to – approach a class. Order and control are major anxieties for rookie teachers:

> As pupils, most of us have had direct experience of teachers who lost control of their classes. Images of riotous behaviour, even mob rule, can easily be brought to mind. ... The idea of being on the receiving end of this is indeed frightening. 'Will I be able to control them?' is a question young teachers often ask and even more often worry about. They are right to do so. (Desforges, 1995:180-181)

Whilst school-based teaching practice gives teachers-in-training insights into how teachers deal with students, they do not see experienced teachers' first encounters with their students at the beginning of the school year. Yet this is so important:

> The success or failure of a whole year may rest on the impressions created, the ethos, the rules and relationships established during the first two or three weeks in September. And that is one reason why many teachers see it as a private matter rather than something to be observed and analysed. (Wragg and Wood, 1994: 116)

The first trio of films in this chapter come from the 1950s and 1960s. Each film is based on a book written by a real world teacher, and features the resilient charismatic teachers Richard Dadier, John Saunders and Mark Thackeray.

Blackboard Jungle

Blackboard Jungle was adapted from the first novel by Evan Hunter, a young writer who later became famous under the pseudonym Ed McBain. It caused such outrage on its screening at the 1955 Venice Film Festival that the American Ambassador to Italy put pressure on the Italian authorities to have the film withdrawn (*Daily Telegraph*: 01/09/55, 13/09/55). In America, the *Hollywood Reporter* (Moffit: 28/02/55) claimed:

> It surrenders the audience to feelings few movies have dared unleash before – the fiercely exhilarating sense of power that comes with the ability to flout authority, the giddy intoxication that comes with an un-restrained display of insolence, the exalting sense of egoistical fulfil-ment when the impoverished and underprivileged fight their way, not to equality, but to mastery over other elements of society.

This flouting of authority and display of unrestrained insolence is evident from the first meeting between the students at North Manual High School and Richard Dadier. Richard Dadier enters his classroom as the students slowly settle themselves, all except West, whom he has to tell to sit down. After going round the classroom giving out cards, Richard Dadier moves to the blackboard and begins to write some information, including his name, on the board. A baseball is thrown at the board and, dramatically, its impact smudges his name. He pauses, there is silence, and he and the class look at one another. Using humour to defuse the situation, he responds: 'Whoever threw that, you'll never pitch for the Yanks, boy'.

The interaction with key students which follows reinforces the importance of respect. He tells them to call him Mr Dadier. He tries to establish more classroom ground rules, for example, there should be no calling out; students should raise their hands if they want to contribute. But they keep testing him out, and he has another confrontation with West, when he asks him to take his hat off. The tension begins to tell: Richard Dadier mops his brow a couple of times, and is particularly embarrassed about his reaction to Santini, referred to by another of the students, Miller, as an 'idiot boy'. At the end of the lesson, Richard Dadier calls Miller back and tries to persuade him onto his side. As Miller leaves, Richard Dadier is seen throwing the baseball ball up and down, a look of relief on his face.

Blackboard Jungle was based on Evan Hunter's own traumatic ex-periences of teaching in a South Bronx vocational school:

> It was the fall of 1950 and I hated it. I was very idealistic when I went in there. I thought I'm going to give these kids who want to be motor mechanics Shakespeare and they are going to appreciate it and they weren't buying it. I went home in tears night after night. So I quit. (Fountain and Anuja, *G2*, 12/04/04)

Sidney Poitier, who played the part of the student Miller, talked about people describing the film as un-American and a misrepresentation of American high school education:

> It was a vocational school in New York City, a school for the incor-rigibles and the kids who weren't doing too well. The message com-ing loud and clear from these critics of our film was, 'This wasn't us.' But Richard Brooks, the film's director, had a different message: 'Yes it is. This is 'us' too.' (Poitier, 2000: 97-98)

Richard Dadier has a set of values, coupled with faith in American youth despite their background of dysfunctional families upset by the war. The problems the students have originate outside the classroom: gang life is taking the place of family life, and there is little prospect of employment after school. Delinquent behaviour boils over into schools, not just among the students but also in violent attacks on teachers, both physical and verbal.

In his class, Richard Dadier spots a potential powerful ally in Miller, a more suitable leader of the students than West, who is a bully and is determined to make the lives of both Richard Dadier and his wife a misery. Richard Dadier gains Miller's trust through using extra-curri-cular activities as a tool, such as involving him in the school's Christ-mas production. Miller thus sees 'Teach' as a good, decent guy.

Richard Dadier attempts to find the inspiration and guidance he seeks from his old college professor, who tries to tempt him away from his 'jungle' to a more co-operative school, a move his wife would welcome. However, Richard Dadier decides to take one more crack at his 'jungle' and, with West eventually vanquished and Miller's support gained, he decides to stay at the school.

Although this film about a resilient charismatic teacher may appear dated today, its lasting impression is clear from the continued references to it as a benchmark for fictional portrayals of schools. It even received a mention in Parliament:

> What I remember vividly from originally watching that film, which was set in the United States, it was like watching a kind of science fiction movie. Lunatic kids, not taking any notice of their teacher, carrying knives to school. It was literally, like looking at a science fiction film. It is no longer science fiction. (Puttnam, 09/02/00)

Spare the Rod

The English equivalent of *Blackboard Jungle*, *Spare the Rod* was based on a book written by Michael Croft in 1954 about his own experiences as a teacher, but a seven-year censorship controversy meant that the film was not distributed until 1961. Max Bygraves' belief in the book led him to put his own money into the film (*Observer*, 04/06/61). The son of a docker, Bygraves had been to a school like the one in Michael Croft's book. He was determined that the book should be filmed, and invested his life savings, £48,000, in the project (*Bryanston Newsletter*, 04/05/61). He starred as John Saunders, a crusader against corporal punishment who finds himself in the tough, working-class Worrell Street School in the east end of London:

> Croft's purpose was to draw attention to the grave and complex problems facing many teachers at the present time 'whose work I have tried to describe sympathetically and faithfully'. Despite his good intentions, the leading teachers' unions were far from pleased and expressed considerable disapproval and anger in the pages of their professional journals. (Aldgate, 1995: 14)

Chaos greets John Saunders and headteacher Mr Jenkins as they enter the classroom. Mr Jenkins attempts to take control, but is overcome by a fit of coughing, so that John Saunders has to quieten the class down. Once he recovers, Mr Jenkins explains that Mr Saunders is an ex-navy man who is used to dealing with troublemakers of the likes of this class. He decides that the first lesson of the day will be arithmetic, sets some problems, and departs. John Saunders sits down attentively at the teacher's desk. Cautiously he interrupts the students and tries to strike up a conversation along the lines of 'I expect you're wondering what sort of sport I am' and vice versa. The response to this is a book hurled at the desk leg, accompanied by a take-off of his accent. 'I'll ignore that remark for the moment' is his response.

John Saunders tries again: he wants them to work with him just as the crew and captain of a ship do. He says he is relying on them to help him find his feet, and in return he will do his best to help them with any problems they may have. After taking their names down in the register, the question of monitors arises, and when Mr Saunders suggests a vote, there is uproar. At this point, the headteacher reappears and gives the class their second warning of the morning about bad behaviour. Mr Saunders should not have given them the chance to do something as interesting as voting for monitors – much safer to choose the usual pairs of hands, Harkness and Shrub. He dispatches them to do their first job: checking gym shoes. Harkness cannot resist a little victory signal as he exits the classroom.

In the classroom, as John Saunders slowly begins to make progress with his form, a divisional inspector appears, who informs him that he is the best teacher he has seen for some time. Unfortunately John Saunders' growing confidence is severely dented when he misjudges a situation concerning one of the girls in his class. The subsequent confrontation with the whole class causes him to lose his temper and resort to the cane, something he had vowed never to do. This is swiftly followed by the all-night incarceration by some of the students of Mr Gregory, bully and main support of the headteacher, in an outside toilet.

Convinced that Harkness is behind this, Mr Gregory storms into John Saunders' class. The students react by going on the rampage. In uncovering the true miscreant, John Saunders sides with Harkness, who did not commit the offence, so implying a lack of support for Mr Gregory. This results in his being identified with the students against the authority of the teachers. The headteacher forces John Saunders to resign, albeit with the promise of good references for another school – that is, if he does not give up teaching altogether.

The end of the film provides further conflict for John Saunders. As his students gather round him, the parents of the one black student in his class come to the school gates to thank him for all he has done for their daughter. Once again, he is confused: does their gratitude make him decide to stay in the teaching profession?

According to Aldgate (1995: 27), 'the publicity material which accompanied the film laid great stress on selling it as 'The Film They Tried to Stop":

The film version of his novel of life in a secondary modern school was bound to make the teachers furious. Mr Croft, who has taught in three secondary modern schools, added: 'The school is a bad one and not meant to be typical. When the novel was published I was always being told by speakers at educational conferences that I should have written about a good school with a good staff.' (Shorter, *Daily Telegraph*, 16/05/61)

London County Council banned the film company from using its schools for the film. Members were concerned that 'parents and teachers might think the sort of school to be shown on the screen is typical of one of ours' (*Bryanston Newsletter*, 04/05/61):

This belated (by over six years) version of Michael Croft's novel does not shirk the original's reality, nor its attack on ill-equipped schools, semi-illiterates, the disillusion and brutality of elements in the teaching profession, the sense of perpetual war between these elements and the slum children in their charge. (*Monthly Film Bulletin*, July 1961: 96)

To Sir, With Love

Twelve years after the release of *Blackboard Jungle*, Sidney Poitier crossed the classroom floor from his seat in the back row to the teacher's desk at the front of the class, to become Mark Thackeray in the 1967 film, *To Sir, With Love*. It is based on a true story and written by Edward Braithwaite, a Guyanese ex-serviceman, about teaching in the east end of London. Mark Thackeray had trained as an engineer and as a new and reluctant entrant to the teaching profession, he meets the challenge of undisciplined students by treating them as young adults. But first he must go through the baptism of his first encounter with this new class.

We hear the voice of the teacher calling the register. The camera pans round the classroom to pick up the students and match them to each name. They are engaged in various activities, all of which suggest inattention and/or boredom: doing their make-up, eating or chewing, reading, writing, flicking things. They answer the teacher with 'yeah' or 'hmm'. Sometimes the teacher has to repeat a name. There is a general atmosphere of a class half asleep, many lolling across their desks or sitting with their feet up on them. After he has taken the register, Mark Thackeray tries to begin the lesson. He asks the students to read a passage of writing from one of their school books, so that he can gauge what they know. This does not start promisingly, as the first boy has to be helped by the student sitting next to him. The next reads a problem from a mathematics textbook, the next an excerpt from an erotic paperback. Mark Thackeray is distracted during this by two students at the back of the class with their heads inside their desks and he goes over to them. They have a small, semi-naked plastic doll which they are examining. He tells them off, and as he returns to the front of the room, one of the desk lids goes down with a bang. There is silence while meaningful looks are exchanged. The reading exercise continues, with another student, Pamela Dare, volunteering to read. She is by far the best reader, and she receives a round of applause from her peers. Mark Thackeray decides to move the lesson on to mathematics. On the subject of weights and measures, one of the boys who had the doll responds with his knowledge of boxing weights, which raises a laugh. Mark Thackeray responds with sarcasm, which the students do not like. There is muttering as he turns to the board.

Mark Thackeray begins his teaching career at this school in London Docks, North Quay Secondary, with a traditional, didactic approach which he quickly abandons. He suspends the limiting, formal curriculum, which he sees as academically irrelevant to his students, and instead practically connects lessons to personal and social development. Because of his treatment as a black man, he knows that life is not fair, and he uses himself as an example that anyone can change. In the best tradition of the resilient charismatic teacher, this becomes his mission. He can empathise with his students because he appreciates what it means to be downtrodden. Patriarch, mentor and guru to the students and their families, he sets rules in the classroom which are also standards for the wider community. Despite his colour, the white parents gradually warm to him and extend friendship to this new teacher.

Throughout his time at the school, Mark Thackeray applies for engineering posts, and when he is finally offered a job, he has to decide about his future. As he sits in his classroom with the job offer in his hand, two students barge in and inform him that they will be in his class the following academic year. Faced with another class like the one he has just said goodbye to, Mark Thackeray comes to his decision. In his biography, Sidney Poitier (2000) reflected:

> In the end, though, he succeeded in helping his students to see themselves in this new life as valuable, useful human beings with impressive potential. Just as this transformation came about, a new opportunity opened up for him. ... He said no to the dream he had hoped for and stayed to help the next class of disadvantaged students. (p189)

This decision to remain at the chalkface endorses the observation made by Goodlad (1990):

> We have been inclined, many of us, to think of a profession as a calling, conjuring up images of idealistic young men and women preparing themselves to serve God or humankind or both. At times, teaching is so envisioned and depicted as in the movie *Stand and Deliver* ... (p15)

The next three charismatic teachers all have in common their initiation of their respective classes into what Martin (1984:11) terms the 'arcane': Jean Brodie into the usually off-limits sexual and political awareness, Jaime Escalante into the mysteries of calculus and John Keating into the obscurities of poetry.

The Prime of Miss Jean Brodie

This is the story of a romantic, outspoken, eccentric teacher who works in an exclusive girls' school in Edinburgh, the Marcia Blane Academy, captivating her students with her outrageous views on politics, life and love. Jean Brodie depends on personal charisma, and treats her students as clean slates to be written on, particularly her quartet of girls: Sandy, Jenny, Monica and Mary.

From the first day of the new academic year, she wastes no time in setting out her agenda. The students enter the classroom and one waits by the door to warn of Miss Brodie's approach. On entering, she immediately makes some comment on how wide the window has been opened: according to her, more than six inches is vulgar. She moves to the teacher's desk and begins the lesson with administration. There are two new students in the form this academic year. Emily Carstairs, the girl guide, is quickly dismissed, whereas Mary McGregor is received more warmly. It is Jean Brodie's interest in Mary which will end in tragedy for the student. It does not matter that Mary, unlike Emily, has no interests, because one of Miss Brodie's objectives is to provide her students with interests.

She launches into what might be termed her 'dedication speech' (the usual truisms trotted out at the beginning of each academic year), in which she informs the girls that she is in the business of putting old heads on young shoulders and that her pupils are the *crème de la crème*. Give her a girl at an impressionable age and she is Miss Brodie's for life. The girls are her vocation. She warns the two new girls that they might hear Miss Brodie's teaching methods decried in some quarters, because she aims to challenge the status quo and not die of petrification. She tells the students to prop up their books on their desks, in case of 'intruders'. To an outsider, the class is doing history: in reality, Miss Brodie is telling the students about her Italian holiday. She takes out a poster of a painting by Giotto and pins it over the one of Stanley Baldwin, the headteacher's hero, at the back of the classroom. Miss Brodie then appears to fall to reminiscing, talking about one of her ex-lovers. But she does not go too far away, as she reprimands one of the students for having her sleeves rolled up: is the girl thinking of doing a day's washing? She will not have anything to do with girls who roll their sleeves up: 'We are civilised beings,' she tells her.

Miss Brodie continues with her personal story, which makes Monica cry. But the class is interrupted by the arrival of the headteacher, Miss McKay, who is concerned to find a student crying over a history lesson. Miss Brodie improvises that the class are studying the Battle of Flodden, a moving episode in Scottish history. This appears to mollify the headteacher, who welcomes the students back in the new term and encourages them all to work hard this year. She is looking forward to their essays on what they did during their holidays. Making to leave the classroom, she notices that her poster has been replaced with another. As she leaves the room she gives Miss Brodie a wan smile. Miss Brodie congratulates Monica on not giving the game away.

With the Brodie set, their teacher has an over-familiar relationship. She shares a wealth of enriching extra-curricular activities – picnics, teas, weekends away and trips to the opera. She moulds the girls in her own image, indoctrinating them and making them different from the rest of their peers, and this ultimately creates conflict in the school:

> Jean Brodie appeals to a popular belief that the truly memorable teacher is the one who cultivates our individuality and helps us to discover our truest, best, and most original selves, especially as she explicitly sets herself in opposition to the notion of the teacher as one who merely imparts information. (Keroes 1999: 36)

Although Jean Brodie says she is dedicated to goodness, truth and beauty, she undermines authority by subverting the curriculum and ensures her students' discretion through fear and threats. Her teaching methods are disapproved of. Jean Brodie's girls are spoken of as being 'different', but she cares little what colleagues think. Nor is she intimidated by the headteacher, as she was at the school before Miss McKay arrived and considers herself to be well in with the board of governors.

However, Jean Brodie's unorthodox approach has dire consequences, when Mary runs away to fight and die in the Spanish civil war. Eventually the headteacher, keen to oust her because of her teaching methods and her relationships with her students and colleagues, suspends her with the agreement of the governors.

Stand and Deliver

In *Stand and Deliver,* Jaime Escalante, a Bolivian-born computer scientist, decides to give up his well-paid, high-status job in order to teach in a tough high school in an Hispanic neighbourhood in Los Angeles. As a production commissioned by their Public Broadcasting Service network's American Playhouse slot, the story of Jaime Escalante is 'very much in the US TV-movie tradition of true stories with an inspiring social message'.

> The classroom scenes are consequently as near as one can get outside documentary to reproducing Escalante's method, with its use of dramatic examples and its appeal to the students' culture. (Buss, *Times Educational Supplement,* 02/12/88)

Jaime Escalante convinces his class of undisciplined students that education is valuable. The review in *Cineaste* (Cross 1988: 53) describes him as the teacher who will make the students sit up and think: 'Edward James Olmos plays Escalante as an unlikely hero, overweight, tackily dressed, unimpressive looking, the kind of teacher whose attire might garner a few snickers from his students.'

His first encounter with his new class is chaotic. The classroom walls are covered with graffiti, and there are more students than there is classroom furniture to accommodate them. Against a background of student noise, Jaime Escalante, the 'teacher man', tries to overcome the problem by getting some students to change places. His classroom management skills are stretched to the limit. The students try to distract him by asking whether they can have a discussion about sex and feelings. He responds by saying he would then have to set sex for homework. Just as he has settled the class as best as he can, the bell goes – not because it is the end of the lesson but because the students have rigged the school alarm system. Bedlam reigns in the corridor outside the classroom; the principal appears and orders the students back to their lessons. The principal follows Jaime Escalante's class into the room. He is given to standing at the windows, surveying his school population through binoculars. The bell goes again ...

Jaime Escalante is passionate about mathematics and about teaching, particularly disadvantaged students who share his ethnic background and experiences of being one of a minority group. He is a champion of his students, and a man of the people, who wants to drag them out of the ghetto and away from their existing lifestyle. It is his belief that everything is subservient to academic results, and as these improve so does the chance of job prospects and the quality of life as a whole. Consequently he enters his class for the higher examination:

> He's given up a lucrative electronics job just so he can share his love of advanced calculus with the kids and soon, thanks to his vaudeville-style teaching methods, he's persuaded his class of semi-literate chicano gang members to stay in after school for extra lessons. (Wrathnall, *City Limits*, 17-24 November, 1988: 27)

Escalante's Head of Department warns him that because of their socio-economic background, these students will not bounce back if they fail the higher examination he wants them to sit. Her negative attitude makes it clear that she does not understand his wish to extend his students, yet her doubts are valid, as it is the students who will pay if his 'experiment' fails.

In order to make sure they do *not* fail he gives them more time than he does his own family, at a cost to his family and himself. Jaime Escalante works extra hours, gives up his holidays, and eventually hospitalises himself with a heart attack. Even whilst he is in hospital, he sends out work to his students.

> He asks his nurse for a Red Cross card so he can scribble some things. They turn out to be mathematical computations. These are snuck into his calculus class the next day for his students to use as they prepare for the AP [Advanced Placement] exam. The students receive this teaching aid right before Escalante himself walks into class. Two days after his heart attack he's back teaching! He's back for his students. There is something overtly religious about this sense. Escalante has risen from his sick bed to return to his teaching job in two days. A miracle. (Bodnar 1996: 60)

Having entered the students for the Advanced Placement examination, Jaime Escalante is set for his confrontation with the examination board executives, who are racist in their misguided belief that the students could not possibly pass the examination they have sat so accuse them of cheating. For a moment, Jaime Escalante questions his endeavours. He has already had to confront and challenge the parents so he could keep his students in school long enough to graduate. Jaime Escalante's wife 'in the grand tradition of teacher helpmates established by Mrs Chipping in *Goodbye, Mr. Chips*, supplies quiet encouragement' (Weinstein, 1998: 161):

> Jaime Escalante: I don't know why I'm losing sleep over this. I don't need it. You could make twice the money and work less hours and have people treat me with respect.
>
> Signora Escalante: Respect? Jaime, those kids love you.

However, when the students produce the same outstanding results in the re-sit, his conviction to stand alone in a wasteland of prejudice and deliver success at Garfield High School is vindicated. This class is to become the first of many of Jaime Escalante's groups which achieve legendary results in advanced mathematics.

Dead Poets Society

From a passion for mathematics to a passion for English: John Keating believes that poetry is a living thing and this underpins his inspirational approach to his students to pursue individual desires and, by subverting tradition, encourages them to make their lives extraordinary. Handler Spitz (1992) compared John Keating's teaching and learning style with those of his colleagues:

> Rigid, methodical, and demanding, the lab science teacher strides about his domain, inducing admixtures of terror and boredom. McAllister, the latin [sic] master, framed by his chalkboard, repeatedly intones the declension of the simple feminine noun 'aricola'. The maths teacher fixes on precision and punishment. Thus the model is unmistakable: rote learning and conformity to a given norm. Keating, however, instantly punctures this paradigm. (p21)

The class enters, and Mr Keating is seen peeping round the connecting door between the classroom and his office. Once the students have settled themselves, he makes his entry, walking through the room, whistling *The 1812 Overture*. On reaching the door, he encourages them to follow him out. Obviously mystified by this unusual approach, the students get up out of their places. Taking them out of their usual learning environment, he leads them down to the entrance hall to introduce them to poetry. He has a sense of humour which the students nervously respond to. When he asks one of them a question, and a boy, Charlie Dalton, responds wrongly, he pretends that they are on a games show, presses an imaginary bell, shouts 'Ding!' and thanks him for playing. He draws them towards the photographs of old boys of the school which adorn the walls of the entrance hall, and encourages them to lean in and listen to what these people have to say to them. 'Carpe Diem!' he whispers behind the students' backs. 'Seize the day, boys! Make your lives extraordinary!' One of the boys, Todd Anderson, is obviously captivated by this moment.

In his unofficial biography of Robin Williams, Dougan (1998) described how the actor drew on John Campbell, one of his teachers, as inspiration for the character of John Keating:

> 'John Campbell is an abrasive man,' says Williams. 'He was my wrestling coach, a history teacher who basically said history would make a great farce, and that more wars would be hilarious except that massive numbers of people die from the madness.' You can see why Campbell would appeal to Williams in the process of building John Keating's character. (p190)

John Keating is a former student of Welton and has first-hand experience of its stultifying environment, which might explain his rejection of conformity and his being unafraid of taking on the establishment via his unorthodox teaching methods. His inspirational love of poetry causes seven of his class to reinstate an old tradition, the Dead Poets Society, which had been John Keating's brainchild when he was a student at the school.

One of the septet is Neil, a boy who lacks confidence. John Keating teaches him to value himself and his ambitions and this brings him into conflict with his father, who Keating thinks is narrow-minded. John Keating wants the boys to throw off their parents' attitudes and values and urges them to enter into frank communication, rather than confrontation, with their families. Although his father forbids him to take part in a production of *A Midsummer Night's Dream*, Neil disobeys, with the result that he is taken away from the school and eventually commits suicide.

The reality of the responsibility and influence teachers have is reflected in this tragedy. Because of Neil's suicide, John Keating is compelled to leave the school. But he retains the loyalty of many of his English class, who salute their 'Captain' as he leaves his classroom for the last time.

Shiach (cited by Rayner, 1998) is cynical about the film's appeal. He rates it as 'a well-crafted exercise in Hollywood emotionalism ... quite blatant in its attempted manipulation of the sympathies of the spectator' (p195). Dougan (1998) reinforced the film's power to evoke an emotional response in its audiences, describing how spectators were moved to tears by the ending of the film when John Keating collects his personal belongings from his classroom and leaves Welton while his students stand on their desks in tribute to the charismatic teacher who has so powerfully influenced their lives.

Dangerous Minds

The next pair of films moves the charismatic teacher film firmly back into the inner city school, with its problems of juvenile indiscipline of the 1990s.

Dangerous Minds was based on the story of LouAnne Johnson, whose book, *My Posse Don't Do Homework*, was read by the general public and teachers (Mitchell and Weber, 1999). It was later re-issued under the title of the film, and had another spin-off in a weekly one-hour television series.

Like Richard Dadier, John Saunders and Mark Thackeray, LouAnne Johnson is ex-service personnel, an ex-marine. Again, the discipline of her former life conflicts with her task of teaching a group of raucous students who do not want to learn and have come to accept failure as a way of life. As an English teacher at Parkmount High School, she is assigned to the 'Academy School', a polite label for a department of unteachable students.

As she enters the classroom for the first time, music is blaring, students are sitting on desks, talking and rapping, oblivious to her entry. She puts her briefcase on the teacher's desk at the front of the room. Nervously, she smiles and waits, then shouts over the noise to try and get the class's attention. When she gets no response, she moves to a small group and, in an effort to break the ice, asks them what happened to their former teacher. One of the group gets up on her chair and shouts at the rest of the class. The students quieten down, and someone responds: 'Killed the bitch; Emilio ate her'. Emilio, the ringleader of the class, moves menacingly towards Ms Johnson: their former teacher was too ugly to eat, he fed her to his dog, but he'll eat Ms Johnson. She asks him his name, and writes it on the board. The students start to chant.

The scene moves to the class across the landing, who are distracted from their work by the noise. Their teacher chides them – they know what the students next door are like. The scene moves back to Ms Johnson's classroom, with she and Emilio confronting one another at the front of the class, indicating that the class must choose either her or him. Eventually she picks up her briefcase and exits. The student chuck paper balls after her.

She walks across the landing to the other classroom, opens the door and lets it slam shut. Her teaching friend, Griffith, emerges, and LouAnne Johnson demands to know what happened to the previous teacher – a breakdown? Apparently she quit before her breakdown. These kids have a lot of 'social problems', and in response to her claim that she cannot teach them, her friend replies: 'All you've got to do is get their attention.' As if to reinforce the point, he returns to his own classroom whistling, and calls, 'I'm back!' A close-up shot records her reflecting on his words.

The scene moves to her at home reading a book, *Assertive Discipline*, at her desk, the state of which implies that she has spent much soul-searching over how to tackle this class. She reads out loud, realises she has done precisely what the book recommended and that it was a flop. She laughs and discards the book. Her head in her hands, Lou-Anne Johnson broods on the situation. This continues in bed, where she suddenly sits up and moves to the wardrobe: 'OK, you little bastards!' she mutters.

Abandoning the female equivalent of the traditional teacher uniform of elbow-padded tweed jackets and brogues, that of the dowdy suit and prim blouse, LouAnne Johnson grabs their attention by wearing a leather jacket and jeans. Given a class which has already caused three teachers to quit, she quickly discovers that conventional teaching methods will not work with them. She develops an alternative style, which incorporates impressing the class with her karate skills, bribing them with candy bars to work, and using gimmicks such as the Dylan/Dylan competition, where she accesses poetry by means of song lyrics.

In wanting to break the student cycle of not finishing school, Lou-Anne Johnson shows that responsibility for her students does not stop at the classroom door. She goes to their homes and confronts their parents:

> Whenever these kids do face a crisis – an unwanted pregnancy, the threat of violence, or dropping out of school – LouAnne invades their homes and private lives, using the opportunity to win the kids' allegiance or draw attention to her own divorce, physical abuse, or sense of despair. (Giroux, 2002: 151)

But she constantly finds herself defeated and demoralised by the lives of her students. Having got Emilio on her side, she discovers that her own moral code cannot be imposed on the boy, whose brief life of violence ends in tragedy. Discovering that Emilio sought help from the principal but was denied access to him proves to be the last straw, and LouAnne Johnson hands in her notice. It is at this point that her students turn the tables on her and bribe her to stay, employing the same sort of gimmickery that she has used on them. On hearing of the students' tactics to make LouAnne Johnson change her mind and stay at the school Griffith, who was instrumental in getting her the job in the first place, is heard to whisper, 'That ought to do it!'

In an interview for *Film Review* (Rynning, February 1996), Michelle Pfeiffer claimed the film showed what it was like to be a student in the 1990s and explained why she took the starring role in *Dangerous Minds*: 'It's a stirring account of the education crisis in America. ... I've been pretty distraught about the state of education lately, that's why I was drawn to the project.' (p12) However, the review in the *Times Educational Supplement* (Buss, 26/01/96) was more sceptical:

> Simple, isn't it? If Michelle Pfeiffer can cope that easily with a class of angry black and Hispanic kids from north California, only a very poor teacher surely, would fail to do the same in Birmingham or Bermondsey.

To Sir, With Love 2

London was the setting for the 1960s film *To Sir, With Love*. The film *To Sir, With Love 2* (1996) reunites the audience with Mark Thackeray, who returns to North Quay Secondary School for a party to mark his retirement. Standing under a banner bearing the words 'To Sir, with 30 years of Love' he thanks the assembled gathering, which includes ex-students Pamela Dare and Babs Pegg, for the privilege of teaching the 900 children he has been involved with – as he puts it: 'From Sir, with very much love'. But he is not retiring – he is moving to a school in Chicago.

His first encounters with his new class remind teachers that discipline is an ongoing issue throughout their career – that relationships have to be rebuilt at the start of each academic year (Wragg and Wood, 1994). Thirty years on from his first days in the classroom in England, Mark Thackeray begins a new phase of his teaching career in an American classroom.

Mark Thackeray enters to music and chaos. It is the same stereotypical student body he encounters 30 years ago, only updated to suit the 1990s. Some students are dancing, some are fighting, one is smoking. He tries to speak over the noise. He wades into the fighters, turns the music off and slowly order is restored: the class is in session. He begins by asking them to check their schedules to see if they are in the right room. This has the effect of making the students rush for the door – he should know better by now – but he gets there first and returns them to their seats. As they lounge behind their desks, he explains the regime, and that it is still based on respect. The students are not to call him 'dude' or 'bro' or 'man' but 'Mr Thackeray' or 'Sir'.

A student comes in late, and he and Mr Thackeray exchange glances. This is another student who will not show the respect Mr Thackeray requires, so the teacher pursues him. The student responds that Mr Thackeray must be new; he does not even look as if he comes from round here. Mr Thackeray explains that he is from England and this information engages the other students. He uses the disruption to make a teaching point about where he comes from. The camera pans round the students as they respond. The student warns the others that this brother is trying to mess with their heads already. 'That's what I'm here for,' agrees Mr Thackeray. He reminds the student that he asked him to say his name, and then he is going to ask him to sit down. The student ignores the first instruction, goes and sits down and remarks that it is hot in the classroom. A debate ensues about opening the windows and many of the students get out of their seats again and go to the back of the room to open them. After exchanging a meaningful glance with Mr Thackeray, the ringleader exits, and behind the close-up of Mark Thackeray, the classroom is in chaos once more.

But not for long. Thackeray takes his students on to the streets of Chicago, where he teaches them respect and courtesy in approaching and talking to members of the public. He finds part-time jobs for students in his class. Evie, a would-be journalist, gets a post at the local newspaper and uses her access to the archives to track down Mark Thackeray's lost love. He is reunited with her, and meets the son he never knew he had. He also gets caught up in the local gun culture problem, and is temporarily suspended from school when he obstructs the police in their enquiries. What is more, he nearly gets himself shot when he tries to get to the bottom of what is going on among some of his students.

Mark Thackeray eventually wins round yet another set of unteachable students. At graduation, he is joined by his son to watch his class leave school. At the party afterwards, his students are keen to know if it is true that he will be going back to England. Mark Thackeray feels that in England he was put out to pasture. He has decided that John Adams High School in Chicago *is* the pasture.

187

A genre must evolve in order to maintain audience interest. The final two films discussed in this chapter break new ground. Written by a real teacher, *187* initially appears to follow the storyline of the resilient charismatic teacher. However, 'Although [*187*] may at times brush shoulders with its closest cousin, the anodyne *Dangerous Minds*, the bullies are not romanticised – you can tell they'd do more than just steal your lunch money' (Gilbey, *Independent*, 11/09/97).

The writer of *187*, Scott Yagemann, initially made his living by substitute (supply) teaching in Los Angeles in some of the toughest schools. When one student threatened to kill him, he thought it was just another bullying tactic, until he found out that the student had stabbed a colleague the previous term. This might have signified the end of a career for many, but he saw his chance to write a film based on his experiences of teaching (Steen, *The Guide*, 7-13 March, 1998):

> Outta the way Mr Chips. And if you see Miss Jean Brodie, tell her to go take a flying leap. When a film director makes a movie about school these days, tweeds are out. (Klein, *Times Educational Supplement*, 12/09/97)

Trevor Garfield looks like the resilient charismatic teacher, battling against the ignorance and indifference of the inner city state school. Finding a textbook across which the police code for murder, *187*, is scrawled, he suspects a threat on his life from an ex-student. Fifteen months after the predicted vicious attack takes place, he moves to another school which makes his former place of employment look like Eton (Giroux, 2002).

It is not surprising that Trevor Garfield's first encounter with his students makes him nervous. Once in the classroom, he goes to the teacher's desk, gets his notes out of his briefcase, and uses his asthma inhaler. He begins to write some notes on the board. There is noise from the class behind him, who are out of focus. He turns to address them; they remain out of focus to him. He begins to talk over their noise about what he has written on the board.

At last the class comes into focus. As he turns and begins to write on the board again, his chalk breaks. The students tell him he will find more in the teacher's desk. Opening one of the drawers, he finds a gun – just as another teacher turns up. Apparently Trevor Garfield is in the wrong room. In his distress he has not noticed that the walls are covered with displays to do with history. The history teacher whose room it is points across the playground to the room Trevor Garfield should be in. Textbooks are being thrown out of the windows, to lie in the dust and flutter in the breeze. So he has to summon up the courage to enter his classroom, where the students appear menacing and disaffected. One student is standing by the windows, and Trevor Garfield moves towards him and looks out at the books. He asks the boy to do him a favour and go outside and pick the books up. The student refuses. The teacher pursues the matter, but the student is unrepentant; he is already on some sort of tagging system, implying that he has been in serious trouble before, and there are no other disciplinary measures which can be taken against him. He is not afraid of Mr Garfield, who is nothing but a substitute teacher. After this additional insult, the teacher puts the student on report.

As he goes over to the student's desk to give him the piece of paper, he tells the class that this room is their sanctuary and they should respect it. As he hands the report slip to the student he tells him pointedly that he is a real teacher. The student gets up to leave, and Mr Garfield, thinking that the matter has been dealt with, turns to the rest of the class and asks who would like to help him pick up the books. As the student on report reaches the classroom door, he rolls up the report slip and throws it at Mr Garfield, 'stabbing' him in the back with it. The students laugh at what they perceive to be an over-reaction.

As the film proceeds, it is hard to tell how much Trevor Garfield is being tipped over the edge. Suspicion falls on him for the death of a student, and when his classroom, his car and his house are trashed, he takes the law into his own hands by playing a game of Russian roulette with the student who is his greatest 'enemy':

> Ironically, the movie virtually rebukes anyone who would defend teachers by citing horrifying conditions, the inhumanity of the students, and the infrequent victories which can't stem the tide of failures. Since the hero ultimately turns on those he thinks he's trying

to save, the message thoroughly undercuts its pro-teaching stance. (Dougherty, *Sight and Sound*, September 1997: 53)

Nevertheless, an attempt is made at the end of the film to re-awaken sympathy for this teacher when one of his students pays tribute to him:

> He once told me that you can't blame everything on your environment but I think you can push a good teacher too far and he'll go bad like anyone else. I don't know if Mr G done all those bad things but what I do know is that teachers don't get no respect. I'm up here today because of him. He was there for me when nobody else was. Thing is, I should have been there for him too.

As she speaks, a former colleague is seen tearing her framed teacher qualification off the wall and throwing it in the bin. The credits roll, and provide the following information:

> One in nine teachers has been attacked in school.
> Ninety five per cent of those attacks were committed by students. (Metropolitan Life Survey)
> A teacher wrote this movie.

The director, Kevin Reynolds, explained the ethos underpinning the story-line of *187* and how the ending differs so significantly from all the earlier films about resilient charismatic teachers:

> Movies like *Dangerous Minds* allow you to walk out of the picture feeling good about yourself, because they have a nice happy ending. We didn't want to let the audience off the hook, we wanted to rub it in their faces, to say, 'This is what's happening, you'd better address it.' (Bradshaw, *Time Out*, 10-17 September, 1997)

And, as Allister Harry comments, one way of addressing the problem of inner city students out of control is 'to have them killed – by their teacher. The cinematic exploration of the relationship between education and the inner city, so sensitively portrayed by director, Richard Brooks in *Blackboard Jungle* forty years ago, has regressed to nihilism' (1997b: 15). Thus Trevor Garfield 'transforms no one and triumphs not at all' (Keroes, 1999: 134).

Mona Lisa Smile

In 2003, the charismatic teacher film returned. The character is Katherine Watson, a bohemian Californian who, in the early 1950s, takes up a post at Wellesley, a conservative girls only college. Obviously appointed for her brains rather than her pedigree, Katherine Watson is a teacher who, in the mould of Jean Brodie and John Keating, wants to make a difference rather than fit in, but who remains mistress of her own fate in defiance of the school's leadership team.

Wellesley is arguably 'depicted with handy distortion as a finishing school in all but name' (Robey, *Daily Telegraph*, 12/03/04), but this is not one of those 'glorified finishing schools' (Stein, *The Eye*, 06/03/04). It is one of seven schools established in the late nineteenth century to educate the sisters and daughters of men who then attended the boys only Ivy League schools. Into this rarefied atmosphere steps Katherine Watson as the latest member of the Art Department.

As she enters the lecture theatre for her first appearance, her box of slides is taken out of her hands by efficient students. She recovers, and introduces the course as the History of Art 100. Are there any questions? Immediately, 'Your name?' rings out. This time she is more prepared: 'Why don't you go first?' The student and she exchange full names. But the student is not finished: '*Dr* Watson, I presume?' 'Not yet,' replies Katherine Watson. She stops any further conversation by asking for the lights ... but once again, she has been anticipated – they are off before she can finish the sentence.

She introduces the first slide, but is interrupted by a student who describes in detail what is depicted. The second slide receives the same response. And so it proceeds: every slide is correctly identified by a different student. The lesson is over in next to no time. Katherine Watson asks for the lights to come back on. All the students have read the course textbook, and she congratulates them on their thorough preparation. But what do to now? Again, one of the students has anticipated the situation and suggests independent study, at which the students begin to pack up and leave. As Katherine Watson lets them go with a wan smile and begins to pack up her things, an observer at the back of the lecture theatre, hidden from view, also makes to leave.

After this baptism of fire, Katherine Watson decides to go 'off syllabus' (Jays, *Sight and Sound*, March 2003: 51). At their next lesson, she presents the students with some slides of modern art, including a picture by herself done 25 years earlier, in order to stimulate a discussion on what *is* art. She follows this up with a visit to a warehouse to view a Jackson Pollock; and then takes apart the mass distribution of Van Gogh's *Sunflowers* via Painting by Numbers kits.

Frustrated with the ideology of femininity that coexists with education in the school, she continues to challenge her students, this time with slides of contemporary adverts which warn them of the sort of lifestyle these young women can expect after they leave school. Among the quartet who impinge most on her life, Betty is the spiteful editor of the school magazine who takes every opportunity to undermine Katherine Watson's approach, until she realises that 1950s femininity is a cage. Although Joan is helped by Katherine Watson to gain a place at law school, she eventually decides to settle for marriage, but on her own terms rather than society's. Giselle has a number of unsatisfactory relationships with men – including a member of staff who subsequently becomes involved with Katherine Watson – before she decides to take education seriously, while Connie perseveres to succeed in both her career and her relationship. And in the background is the person of Katherine Watson, challenging these students to question the norms and values of society.

Inevitably, she pays the price for her unorthodox approach both inside and outside the classroom. At the end of the academic year, when it is announced that the number of students wanting to take the course she teaches is the highest ever, her return to the school is made conditional on her only teaching the approved syllabus, submitting her lesson plans for approval, providing no student counselling, and maintaining professional relationships within the faculty. So Katherine Watson turns her back on all this and leaves for Europe. As the taxi takes her away, her students ride after her on their bicycles – and Betty rides the hardest and the fastest. 'I'll never forget you!' she shouts.

Described as 'a cross between *Dead Poets Society* and *The Prime of Miss Jean Brodie*' (Quinn, *Independent*, 12/03/04), *Mona Lisa Smile* did not receive rave reviews. In the *Guardian*, Peter Bradshaw called the film 'a desperately insincere lite-feminist version of *Dead Poets Society*' (05/03/04). 'Compared to, say, the disruptive pedagogy of *The*

Prime of Miss Jean Brodie this film seems oddly prudent and well mannered' (Jays, *Sight and Sound,* March 2003: 51).

* * *

These charismatic teacher films feature characters who meet their students for the first time with varying degrees of confidence, based on their previous experience or lack of it. I have outlined how their careers develop. The next chapter considers individual teaching and learning styles and pastoral care ethos, relationships with colleagues and with senior management/leadership, as four of the films are analysed by members of the first teacher sample.

Thus everyday classroom teachers such as Larry Liddle and Mary Price are allowed to contribute to educational debate, making them the subject rather than the object of educational discourse. This is seldom the case. Mike Baker (2000a) has argued that teachers have allowed themelves to be talked about rather than do the talking. However, Bailey (2000: 112-113) interprets the current lack of teacher voice in public debate as stemming from teachers having been ignored, being worked on rather than being worked with: 'We neglect the possibility that teachers, assessing past experiences as well as current realities, may have something important to tell us'. And indeed they do.

Chapter 5

The charismatic teacher film often draws on real world teachers' experiences. It is a way of enabling true stories to be heard, particularly those of the resilient charismatic teachers from the genre of the social problem film, 'a subject of considerable debate' (Maland, 1988: 305) because 'in an industry traditionally devoted to providing 'pure entertainment', its advocates propose that films should treat serious issues'. The film industry is a social institution and part of its claim to integrity and topicality is demonstrated via its representation of social problems (Maltby and Craven, 1995).

Blackboard Jungle, To Sir, With Love, Stand and Deliver, and *Dangerous Minds* fall into the true story category. Members of my first teacher sample reflect on these four films. It should be noted that such films may give a more 'truthful' account of a 'problem' area within society than that reported by official sources (Stevenson, 1995):

> It is all to the good that films should interest themselves in the social problems of the day, and contrary to the opinion that entertainment should be synonymous with inanity, it often happens that such films have a high entertainment value. (*The Times*, 18/05/61)

No matter the cost in personal terms to resilient charismatic teachers, whether it be health, finances, or family, they are always professional. They persevere and finish the job they set out to accomplish, thus rescuing the students everybody else has given up on. The colleagues of resilient charismatic teachers conform to an expected set of roles, especially the experienced cynics who are weary of teaching. Together with the leadership team of the school, these teachers appear to be paralysed in the face of the new teacher on the block. And whilst these colleagues might emulate the resilient charismatic teacher's example and have a positive effect on the lives of other problem students in the school, their efforts are ignored: there is no suggestion of a transformation brought about by team-work.

Eventually these teachers must face up to their dilemma: should they leave a job where they are underpaid and their efforts unappreciated by the leadership team of the school, or should they ignore the bureaucracy and continue to struggle on? 'Teachers in films often follow a pattern of initial missionary zeal, crisis, loss of faith, epiphany, and finally renewal of commitment' (Weinstein, 1998: 242).

Jaime Escalante

In an ideal world, an effective teaching style will motivate students to learn. According to Capel *et al* (1995), teaching style comprises teacher behaviour and teaching strategy. Teacher behaviour takes account of elements such as presentation of self, level of enthusiasm, and extent of distance between the teacher and the class. Teaching strategy draws on a variety of teaching methods, for example, chalk and talk/experimental, teacher-directed/student-centred, or content/process-driven, and teachers often use more than one style during a single lesson.

In the ideal world of the charismatic teacher film, teachers can easily find effective ways of motivating students. In the four rough, tough schools which feature in the films all the main characters have done other jobs before coming into teaching, and this affects their ideas about how teaching and learning should proceed in the classroom.

In *Stand and Deliver*, described in chapter four, Jaime Escalante believes that he can boost his students' examination results. Convinced that they have potential, he adopts unconventional teaching methods to produce top students in calculus: 'Maths is the great equalizer,' he tells them. If they work hard, they will succeed. 'Why work on a car when you can design one?' (Cross, *Cineaste*, 1988: 53).

Despite his poor start, by the time Jaime Escalante is seen at the start of his second lesson, quite a lot has happened. The classroom has been cleaned up, the students all have somewhere to sit – and Jaime Escalante has changed too. He stands at the front of the class, dressed as a chef and wielding a meat cleaver. Dramatically chopping an apple in half, he asks the students about the condition of the apples which are on their desks, a portion of which has been taken away. To the girl who informs him that her apple is missing 25 per cent, he asks whether it is true that intelligent people make better lovers. To the student who has eaten the whole of his apple, he says that he will see him in the people's court.

Having introduced the lesson content of fractions and percentages, he is interrupted by the late arrival of two students. The rest of the class watch this potential confrontation with interest. Mr Escalante asks one of them about his knowledge of times tables, and shows him another way of doing the nine times table (a little juvenile for this age). When the bell goes, he sets the class their homework, and gives one of the students his confiscated magazine back with the proviso that he is not to bring it to class again. He detains the two latecomers. Their menacing attitude does not bode well, but as the film moves on to when the class is seen again some time later on, it is obvious that he has got them on his side. He uses bonding games to induce a collaborative atmosphere, before introducing the topic of algebra. Larry Liddle observed:

> He is concerned with raising expectations of pupils to enhance motivation and their work effort. He uses group dynamics and peer pressure to help achieve these goals. This is a very active and demanding approach.

Together, they read out the problem on the board, which concerns the number of girlfriends three people have. Clive Parker picked up on this approach:

> Jaime Escalante presents concepts in a concrete way (apples), he makes them entertaining and relevant to students' experiences (gigolos). He demystifies difficult or abstruse knowledge by showing how common sense it is.

The class is interrupted by the principal and Jaime Escalante's head of department, coming in to observe his teaching. Once again, his interactions with the students are touched with humour. To one of the boys: 'You think you got it, Einstein?' To one of the girls: 'You're going to end up barefoot, pregnant and in the kitchen'. To another boy he blows a kiss. Mary Price commented on these interactions:

He tries to make learning enjoyable, relevant and real, although the examples he uses and the comments he makes are often very personal and not always politically correct!

To the observers, Mr Escalante remarks that it is not that the students are stupid, just that they don't know anything. At this point, one of his best students puts in an appearance and when she gives him the answer to the problem, he welcomes her with open arms. One of the students raises the issue of using mathematics in the real world, to which he responds by asking the observers if the school could arrange for a couple of gigolos to come in for a practical demonstration.

Jaime Escalante's ethos of pastoral care arises out of common experiences with his students on the basis of their shared ethnicity. They in turn recognise his poverty and renovate his car. He knows that academic results improve equality of opportunity through better job prospects. To this end, he has them at his home to tutor them and cooks for them:

He is concerned about the whole pupil – not just the academic subject. Calculus is his subject, but really this is just a way of improving the lot of those in the classrooms. His ambitions go beyond the classroom. (Sally King)

Jaime Escalante is aware that his students have hard lives, and despite appearing tough on the surface he is willing to offer comfort and show concern for their welfare by opening his house and cooking for them, teaching one of his students to drive, and visiting their homes. He visits the restaurant owned by the father of his star student in order to get her back into the classroom:

Jaime Escalante demands an almost obsessive degree of commitment in the study of maths, and is prepared to intervene where he feels home background is unsupportive. Maths is the great equaliser to combat racial prejudice. (Julian Brown)

The first teacher sample's response to Jaime Escalante implies that some of these *reel* life teachers do work hard; in other media such as the popular press, teachers in general are put down most of the time (see the introduction for a discussion of demonisation). Julian Brown commented:

I enjoyed this film the most so far. For a change, it was less focused on the dramatic potential of disruptive pupils than on the fact of their deprivation. The workload issue appals me! This man works extra hours, gives up his holiday and eventually hospitalises himself. Is he a hero or a fool? Or is this an implicit criticism of the system? The issue of lack of finance was welcome and familiar and not often addressed in these films.

Katherine Fox endorsed the relevance of this film to the everyday lives of real teachers:

I think because it was based on fact it did stand out over the other films because there was so much you could grab hold of. The weird thing was, unlike me, he didn't lose his temper and blow up at the kids – he was just very calm and very straightforward. He internalised all the grief, and by internalising it he was the one that ended up with a heart attack. I've no intention of going that way. I have seen an Art teacher drop dead in Assembly because of the amount of work which he actually put into the class and the kids loved him, absolutely loved him, because he bent over backwards for the kids, and basically he just worked himself into the grave. I'm determined not to do that, says she, working a thirteen hour day ...

Jaime Escalante feels he knows better than the more experienced teachers, and they are upset by him. His manner seems smug and quite arrogant and the other teachers are rather hostile, perhaps jealous of his success:

Although the level of interaction was more plausible than in previous films, he was essentially a maverick and a loner. He insists on working his own way to the extent of precipitating the resignation of his departmental head. (Julian Brown)

Clive Parker agreed:

As is often the case in films about 'inspirational' teachers, he seems to be isolated. He meets with antagonism from the establishment and his own colleagues. They are represented as a factor in his students' failure as they are blinkered. There is no sense of a department or a school working as a team.

Jaime Escalante gains respect from his headteacher because he is seen as a visionary:

Jaime Escalante: Students will rise to the level of expectation, Signor Molina.

Mr Molina: What do you need, Mr Escalante?

Jaime Escalante: *Ganas.* That's all we need ... is *ganas.* (*Ganas* means the desire to do something)

Thus, Jaime Escalante gets his own way with comparative ease. His biggest scene of confrontation with those outside the classroom is with the overbearing, officious examination board executives, who do not believe that these students can pass the examination they are entered for with such good results, and therefore decide the students cheated:

> He is an anti-authority figure against the examiners who accuse his students of cheating. He is not concerned with charming people outside the class – only reaching those in it. (Kirsten Scrivener)

The appeal of *Stand and Deliver* may lie in the fact that it was relatively unknown to members of the teacher sample. It was made for American television so would not have been shown in British cinemas. The realism of the film's method of production obviously impressed many of the teacher sample. As Polly Ford said:

> In this film there is a good representation of lots of conflicting things impinging on the teaching, i.e. not enough chairs, kids who don't speak English, internal politics within a department, outside influences on kids' motivation, e.g. parents wanting them to leave, etc. This film felt the most realistic and moved me the most – not a glitzy film star with superhuman powers magically turning kids round purely with their super characters.

But Clive Parker questioned the speed of Jaime Escalante's success:

> There was something deeply puzzling in the way that the students seemed to accept his value system very quickly and see success and failure in his terms. They very quickly seemed eager to live up to his expectations. The alternative values of a subculture (which is how these students seemed to be represented) don't usually crumble so easily. A lifetime of antagonism to the established system is not going to disappear in one semester because of one man.

Fergus Cook reflected:

I suppose trying to portray student development over a number of months in a one-and-three-quarter hour film is bound to give the impression of success without effort.

Katherine Fox likewise acknowledged the effect of *reel* time on the realistic portrayal of the everyday work of teachers:

I've got into this rut of expecting these kids of not doing terribly well, not demanding too much of them, pushing them but not pushing them too far because then that would be turning them off. Suddenly, we've got this situation appearing in the film – these kids who are very similar to the kids in my school – being pushed well beyond their abilities and responding to it. I was thinking, maybe that's a possibility here, something I should be trying to do here – and I am pushing them. We won't know the results yet for a couple of years. Unlike a film it's not over in an hour and a half.

Mark Thackeray

How I wished I had a teacher like Mark Thackeray when I was in high school, someone who recognised the dull, lifeless nature of the official curriculum that was uncaringly and unrelentingly force-fed to us hour after hour, day after day. (Weber and Mitchell, 1995: 132)

As well as classroom teaching, the academic role of the teacher encompasses a variety of activities including lesson preparation, setting and marking homework, assessing student progress, keeping records of attainment, working as part of a subject team, and curriculum planning and development. But the work of the teacher involves more than these activities which underpin the delivery of the curriculum – every teacher is expected to support the pastoral work of the school (Blackburn, 1975).

Some teachers see the welfare of the students as individuals as outside their professional responsibility, the implication being that they are predominantly interested in their subject and therefore in academic excellence. Others are predominantly interested in children and see pastoral care as underpinning everything they do.

According to Clemett and Pearce (1986), pastoral care has a complex tradition in schools, whereby teachers see (or have been expected to see) their role as jointly comprising teaching their subject and caring for their students. The success of children's education is therefore not only judged by examination results and qualifications but also by the personal development and well-being of students. Pastoral care is specifically referred to in the Elton Report of 1989 as promoting values which underpin positive student behaviour (Capel *et al*, 1995).

No specific references to pastoral care appear in government policies published before the 1970s (Hughes, 1980). The development of the large all-ability comprehensive school (see chapter one) put pastoral care on the agenda. From the mid-1970s onwards, schools were organised to ensure that every student would be the specific respon-sibility of a designated member of staff, and thus the form teacher, or tutor, became a key person in the system (Marland, 1989). But pas-toral care is not something set apart under the auspices of the tutor; it is that part of the teaching process which alters the learning environment to meet the needs of individual students so that they have the maximum chance to realise their potential, whatever their socio-economic background (Hamblin, 1978).

Having tried sarcasm and anger in the classroom, in *To Sir With Love* Mark Thackeray decides to begin again and take a completely dif-ferent direction . A course in life skills is to be the order of the day: everything from instruction in courtesy and personal hygiene to dis-cussion on anything the students want to talk about. Mark Thackeray demonstrates modification of the learning environment, and Julian Brown explained how this happened:

> His motivation stems from a deprived background in which educa-tion is the passport to a better life. It is implied that this shared back-ground, transcending racial and cultural differences, facilitates effec-tive communication between pupils and teacher. Sir's only statement of intent in methodology is that he will not lose his temper. When he does (the only concession to his inexperience) this becomes the catalyst he seeks – dumping the curriculum, he talks to the pupils on their own agenda – the ultimate child-centred approach.

Mark Thackeray makes a dramatic entry into the classroom, signal-ling that he has obviously come to a momentous decision about how to proceed with this class. He sweeps the text books off his desk and into the bin: he tells the students that such resources are useless to them. He shares with his students his insight about the way forward: walking up and down the rows of desks, he tells them that he has realised that they are no longer children but will be adults in a few weeks' time, with all the responsibilities that that entails. So things are going to be different from now on. The students are going to learn the rules of adulthood. They are going to treat one another as adults, with respect. They are going to be reasonable with one another, they are going to talk. Mark Thackeray uses student-led discussion of issues which will prepare them to cope with the demands of life outside the classroom:

> He began to make the lessons more relevant to them by allowing discussion of relevant subjects as opposed to academic subjects. (This wouldn't boost their position in the league tables!) (Sally King)

As he gets into his stride, he is interrupted by the late entry of student Pamela Dare. Totally oblivious to the atmosphere Mark Thackeray has created, she witters on about why she is late while she makes her way to her desk. He decides to use her behaviour as a teaching tool to illustrate what he has just been telling the class. He reprimands Pamela: there are two ways to enter a room one like an adult, and the other like a brat, and she has just demonstrated the latter. Pamela gets up and goes out of the room and enters again in what she considers to be a more adult way. The class are suitably impressed.

Thus behavioural and discipline difficulties are dealt with remarkably quickly in the rough, tough schools. Fergus Cook reflected that the film provided:

> A nice reminder that children change – they can be downright irritating, but with consistency they will respond to positive encouragement from teachers. I think the main relevance would centre around *how* he brought about such a transformation. Of course, adolescents of today are far more sophisticated (at least they think they are), but the basic techniques illustrated in the film are still relevant.

However, Sally King disagreed:

> I would argue that pupils today are more difficult to handle than those in this film. A 1990s school consisting of weak pupils mainly rejected from other schools would use much worse language and would be violent and intimidating. The idea of calling the girls 'sluts' would cause outrage. More equipment and resources would be needed to keep the pupils occupied. Yes, a good teacher can capture the imagination of pupils without resources, but this becomes dif-

ficult to sustain week after week. Pupils expect more today in a world of computers, videos, etc.

A lesson on the topic of survival follows. The students are no longer sitting behind their desks in rows but are informally perched on them in a group in front of Mark Thackeray, who is obviously now at ease with this class and is about to demonstrate how to make a salad. When the boys protest about learning to cook – 'That's women's work' – Mr Thackeray makes a practical point that they may well find themselves on their own, and then they will have to cook for themselves. He has no sooner got started when a student comes in late. And she's had to bring her new baby sister with her because their mum has had to go to the doctor's, and she didn't want to miss today. Mark Thackeray encourages the students to make room for the two of them. He continues with his survival training: the students should never be afraid to experiment because even if they are broke they can still eat well. This prompts a question from Babs Pegg about Sir ever having been skint. He responds that he has, many times. The students have come to realise that he and they have far more in common than they once thought: they find this fact scary but nice. Mark Thackeray agrees that it is scary – but that all he is trying to do is teach them truths, his truth. Pamela Dare is captivated as the lesson continues.

> The film again seems to present the commonly held view that good teachers are naturals rather than the product of a training system. Sir is an engineer by background but he is demonstrably a better teacher than the experienced but burnt-out cynics and stereotyped caring members of the staffroom he joins. (Julian Brown)

Clive Parker touched on the issue of the cult of personality – the dedicated teacher winning round and succeeding with even the biggest problem student without sharing good practice and providing collegial support:

> The school as an institution has given up on the students and expects little of them. The film also reinforces the view of teaching as an activity which succeeds or fails on the basis of the outstanding personal qualities of the individual teacher rather than the long-term work of a whole institution. All teachers therefore feel morally obliged to be inspirational 24 hours a day.

In Mark Thackeray's staffroom, there is the usual cast of clichéd characters. There is Mr Weston, the stereotypical cynic, whose eventual conversion is evident in the grudging respect and compliments he pays Mark Thackeray. A former member of the flog 'em first brigade, he pays tribute to the rookie teacher:

> Theo Weston: You're dammed good, you know. You've done wonders for this shower.
>
> Mark Thackeray: Well, thank you. Thank you very much.
>
> Theo Weston: Anybody can be an engineer. But teaching this mob ... well, I wish I had your gift.

There is the new woman teacher, keen and nervous, and she is the love interest. There is the typical bully: the Physical Education teacher, who Mark Thackeray supports in a professional manner over an incident in front of the students. Venetia Todd observed:

> Despite a rather stereotypical portrayal of his colleagues, e.g. new teacher, jaundiced couldn't-care-less attitude of the slightly older one, the practical and supportive one, the typical PE teacher being a bully, etc, this staff warm to him and give him praise at the end.

The viewpoint of Mark Thackeray's abilities as 'the born teacher' is supported by another *reel* colleague, Clinty, the experienced teacher who offers practical support in a motherly way by dispensing tea and sympathy:

> If you must leave, Mark, go to another school. You can't waste a marvellous talent on rotten electronics.

Clinty is the one supportive element of the senior management team, and offers sound advice on how to handle the female student who is infatuated with Mark Thackeray. The headteacher offers no guidance. Initially, he appears won over by Mark Thackeray and sanctions the innovation of educational visits, but when one trip ends in trouble, he exerts his managerial skills for once and suspends any future events.

Whilst *To Sir, With Love* generated some nostalgia in a number of members of the teacher sample, who remembered its release in a time of idealism in the 1960s, Mark Thackeray was not exempt from criticism. Howard Black observed:

Mark Thackeray never seems to be carrying home any work and carries what is possibly the world's thinnest briefcase.

Richard Dadier

But schools are not just about the teacher/student relationship: they are also about teacher/teacher relationships, which operate at two levels. Firstly, there is the relationship with colleagues at the chalk-face, and the one place where teachers can get away from students and let their facades slip is the staffroom. There have always been staffroom cynics, all too ready to give advice and quash the en-thusiasm of those new to teaching (Williams, *TES Friday*, 08/01/99). During their training and when they first start teaching, those new to the profession are often advised by the cynical teacher that it is a good idea to be very strict and distant for the first half-term in order to esta-blish a reputation as a teacher who can control the students. Whilst Waller (1932) maintained that good teachers kept a marked distance, the well-worn piece of advice, 'Don't smile until Christmas', simply does not work for some individuals.

The hardships of the first two or three years in teaching must be accepted by newly qualified teachers as representing a kind of rite of passage. 'Critical incidents' (Measor 1985: 61) directly challenge the teacher's authority. If the teacher maintains control or employs a con-trolled loss of temper, it seems that their standing is strengthened in the eyes of both students, with whom they are likely to develop easier relationships, and other staff, who begin to respect them as fellow professionals. There is reason to believe this is widespread amongst teachers. Staffroom conversation, especially in secondary schools, often consists of anecdotes about the successful conquest of difficult students: 'these are like battle-scars to be shown to colleagues as evidence of how tough it was and how much professional honour is due to them for finally emerging victorious' (Cole, 1985: 98).

University had not trained the mild-mannered, idealistic, ex-second world war veteran Richard Dadier to deal with students such as the ones he encounters in his first teaching post. Cast in the role of per-sonal crusader, who alone out of the staff cares for the wellbeing of the students, he battles against the hostility of his charges and he finally gains their respect.

On the first day of the new academic year, the members of staff have congregated in the school gym. The staffroom cynic, Mr Murdoch, is getting some practice in on a punch bag whilst he chats to a small group of staff gathered round him. One of them is saying that the principal claims there is no discipline problem at the school. Mr Murdoch jokily responds that there is no discipline problem in Alcatraz. Richard Dadier joins the group as other members of staff come up and introduce themselves. Mr Murdoch explains he is getting in shape to defend himself for the coming term. Richard Dadier comments that he makes it sound like a reform school and is warned by another teacher that Mr Murdoch is a cynic. The new maths teacher wanders up and enquires whether Mr Murdoch has any tips for a rookie. He has two: don't be a hero, and never turn your back on the class. After twelve years in teaching, two purple hearts and no salary increase, he describes the purpose of teaching as sitting on the 'garbage' so that women can walk around the city for a couple of hours without being attacked.

This sexist comment attracts the attention of a new woman member of staff, who queries this: there must be some students who want to learn? Mr Murdoch does not answer this question – he is more concerned about the unsuitability of what she is wearing for teaching teenage boys. The conversation is interrupted by the arrival of the principal, who extends a general welcome to the assembled gathering. But Richard Dadier will not let Mr Murdoch off the hook: the students can't all be bad? Why not? is Mr Murdoch's response.

About his choice of career, Richard Dadier says:

> I want to teach. Most of us want to do something creative. I can't be a painter, a writer, or an engineer. But I thought that if I could help to shape young minds, sort of sculpt lives ... by teaching I'd be creating.

Richard Dadier gets Miller involved in the Christmas entertainment which he is directing; he also goes to the garage where Miller works after school. Between them they make a pact that 'neither of us quit', an example of close one-to-one pastoral care. Miller controls this closeness; he will not help Mr Dadier out with the uncooperative students in the class and it takes the teacher longer to get anywhere than it does his *reel* colleagues in the other films. Clive Parker observed:

It is slightly more convincing than some in that Dadier doesn't have instant success – although the change, when it does come, comes as a sudden turnaround of the whole group.

Some months into Richard Dadier's first year of teaching, a particularly nasty incident occurs to one of his colleagues. Having foolishly brought his precious collection of jazz records into school for a lesson, the maths teacher sees it destroyed by the class Richard Dadier teaches for English. Mr Dadier arrives on the scene just after the chaos has abated, and has instigated a collection from the class in order to replace the records. In the staffroom, Mr Murdoch reports that the punishment the principal meted out to the class was to get them all into the hall and make them write out 500 times: 'I respect private property'. At this point, Richard Dadier comes into the staffroom and says he hasn't got any money for his collection yet. Suggestions on how to punish these students more effectively are offered. The carpentry teacher suggests rigging up an electric chair. Mr Murdoch replies that somehow the carpentry teacher would end up in it first: the solution is to clobber them. Venetia Todd commented:

> Richard Dadier appears to present quite an orthodox approach to his teaching. He wants to be a teacher but finds his faith stretched to the limit. 'I've been beaten up but I'm not beaten' – the incident makes him even more determined to succeed. He is desperate to find a method of reaching the kids – it becomes his personal challenge. He even refuses the offer of a new job in a better school.

Mr Dadier loses his temper with Mr Murdoch. He tells him that the students are used to being clobbered and that they understand this form of punishment because they get it at home and on the street. One of the woman teachers pipes up that she doesn't know what all this has to do with teaching, as she has had no trouble with the students. This is Richard Dadier's cue to turn on all his colleagues: whilst Mr Murdoch is a clobberer, she is a slobberer because she pleads with the boys to be nice to her because she is a pleasant woman just trying to do her job. The carpentry teacher plays on the fact that he is a war veteran and therefore begs for the boys' sympathy: he doesn't care whether they learn anything, only that he keeps his job. The social science teacher is a slumberer: he makes sounds like a teacher but nobody, neither the students nor the staff nor the man himself, listens. Returning to Mr Murdoch, Richard Dadier labels him as a grumbler too, because he hates the students.

So what is Richard Dadier? demands Mr Murdoch. Dadier replies that he is a fumbler – he's doing no better than the rest of the staff. The students do not want to learn, so just what is the way to reach them? Eventually, in the best traditions of the charismatic teacher film, Richard Dadier finds the way to reach his students. Effective teaching and learning require willingness to experiment with a wide range of teaching methods in the attempt to challenge students, who should not be trapped by teachers' expectations. Kirsten Scrivener commented on Richard Dadier's experiences:

> The idea of finding a stimulus that catches the class's attention is very valuable to remember. Also very good was his sudden new insight into Miller – when he hears Miller's group singing wonderfully. It's so easy to get into a rut – if one isn't careful – of having lower expectations of a pupil because of how they perform in your subject and them being amazed at seeing them doing brilliantly in a different context.

Ultimately, Mr Murdoch comes round:

> You got through to them. And those same kids, when they came into my class, a little of your momentum carried over and all of a sudden, I wanted to get through to them too. That was a big day for me.

The changing nature of reality arguably affected the reactions of most of the teacher sample to the dated *Blackboard Jungle*, which is better known and loved for its theme tune.

LouAnne Johnson

The other level of the teacher/teacher relationship involves the members of the senior management team or, increasingly nowadays, the senior leadership team. The role of the day-to-day running of a school once played by the local education authority has been taken on by the headteacher, and this has led to greater administrative, financial and managerial tasks. Consequently, there has been development of a team who help share the workload. Akin to a managing director of a large firm, the headteacher advises the board of directors, the governors of the school. The paternal culture (as portrayed by Mr Wakefield and Brian Stimpson, discussed in chapter one) has thus been reconstructed as managerial, and this has arguably compromised the role as educational leader of the school and distanced staff (Burgess, 1984). Whereas headteachers and their deputies were once socialised within the education sector's values, they are now trained in the generic field of management, and together with heads of department have become line managers. LouAnne Johnson demonstrates in *Dangerous Minds* what can happen when conflict arises between those at the chalkface on a daily basis and those who have left such days behind.

After her first encounter with her new class, the 'bastards' are sure of a big surprise: 'Reinventing herself as a military officer on leave, she further qualifies her new 'tough' no-nonsense look by informing her students she is an ex-marine who knows karate' (Giroux, 2002: 151). But this is not the only attention-grabbing strategy she employs:

> She starts everyone with an 'A' grade and it's up to them to keep it – a good ploy. She seeks a curriculum that will interest them, i.e. she soon realises 'let's conjugate a verb' does not work, and looks for gimmicks to gain their attention, e.g. when considering how to present the poetry package. (I liked the Dylan/Dylan competition.) (Venetia Todd)

Kirsten Scrivener was less impressed with LouAnne Johnson's teaching methods and touched on her use of consumerism:

> Lessons aren't planned, they just come in a flash of inspiration as she sits around in her attractive home and are based on bribery – how long can you hold people's interest with chocolate bars?

Katherine Fox described how she took LouAnne Johnson's approach and adapted it for her own use in the classroom:

> I've got a particularly difficult year 8, approximate reading age from six to about twelve. It's very hard to get them to focus on anything – trying to get them to do homework is a nightmare. So we started doing some project work, and I thought, 'Let's use the old candy bar as a reward.' Rather than using little candy bars, I bought a big Galaxy – eat enough to make you sick sort of job. That was for the person who did the best project, and we got a lot more kids doing it. From that point of view, the approach worked. I tried it again about a month later and not as many kids tried. I haven't done it since. It worked initially because it was quite interesting. The thing was, word of it got

around the school and all the students were asking, 'Do we get chocolate for this?' I did use it with a year 10 group. It varied how [well] it worked. I didn't continue because it lost its impact after the first or second try. So, yes, word spread around and I got a lot more homework out of kids anyway, even though there were no candy bars up for grabs. It had a slight knock-on effect.

LouAnne Johnson blurs the distinction between teaching and social work, as she appears to have unlimited time and freedom to visit students' homes, take a student out to a restaurant, and even have one to stay overnight. Being recently divorced, she has an impoverished private life, so finds both her professional and emotional fulfilment in her students. Her star students, Raul and Callie, the winners of the Dylan/Dylan competition, both fall foul of the educational system: Raul is temporarily suspended because of a fight, and Callie is expected to leave because she is pregnant. LouAnne Johnson attempts to convince both sets of parents of their children's potential. For Polly Ford, *Dangerous Minds* was:

> Another example of a film where the only good teacher is one who spends all their free time doing social work, home visits, etc, etc for the students – the underlying idea being that you're not a good teacher if you don't do all these things.

LouAnne Johnson forms relationships with 'whole people'; she has a concern for students as people rather than just vessels for knowledge. She goes to students' houses:

> She wants to care for each one individually and seems to have unlimited time to do that during, and after, school time. (Doesn't she have a life?) She seems quite hot on equal ops, however, encouraging the pregnant girl to stay on and valuing the often-undervalued Mexican students. (Joyce Carey)

She comes into conflict with members of the senior management team over her educational ideology, and in particular the principal, Mr Grandy, ' an uptight bloodless bureaucrat, a professional wannabe whose only interest appears to be enforcing school rules (Hollywood's favourite stereotype for black principals)' (Giroux, 2002: 156).

LouAnne Johnson has gained some semblance of order over her class through her use of karate, plus the novel idea of awarding 'A' grades to students at the start of the course, which they must strive to keep. She is attempting to teach them parts of speech, utilising the sentence, 'We choose to die'. It is obvious that she is not making much progress, and one of her students explains that the class is not used to such lesson content; they have been restricted to reading what appears to be a 'trashy' novel (*My Darling, My Hamburger*). LouAnne Johnson is perusing this book when the deputy principal appears at the classroom door, and asks her to stop by the principal's office before the next lesson. This elicits the predictable reaction from the students: whistling, cat calls, etc and LouAnne Johnson pulls a mock 'I'm dreading this' face. As Joyce Carey observed:

> Yet again, we have the image of the teacher left to get on with it on their own. The lack of any support system within the school is very unprofessional, therefore it's difficult to write about professional relationships since there really aren't any. (Where's her HOD?)

She makes her way to the principal's office, her head deep in the offensive book, borrowed from a student. She is so engrossed that she walks in on the principal in the middle of a telephone conversation. He immediately puts up his hand to signal that she should withdraw. On putting down the receiver, he patronisingly informs her that his room is an office and people must knock before they enter. Having finally seated herself in front of the principal and beside the deputy principal, LouAnne Johnson is subjected to yet more patronising treatment when the principal informs her that as a new teacher, she doesn't know that teaching karate is against school policy, as an injury could precipitate a law suit. Teachers must follow the curriculum as dictated by the board. LouAnne Johnson responds by informing the principal that it is almost impossible to do this when her students do not even know what a verb is. The deputy principal steps in with a second allegation concerning LouAnne Johnson's unsatisfactory teaching methods – surely there is a better way to teach verbs than using a sentence such as the one she saw on the blackboard when she came into her classroom.

LouAnne Johnson is quick to agree, but says she needed a sentence which would get her students' attention. Warming to her theme, she continues that what she has taught has got to be better than the novel she is reading. The principal remains straight-faced as he informs her that the book is the approved curriculum for her class: she must go along with the school's policies, even if she doesn't agree with them. LouAnne Johnson responds with a muted verbal assent and slight nod of the head.

Thus she is reprimanded early on for criticising the existing curriculum, but soon learns to stand up for herself and her ideals. The principal fails to understand that it almost impossible to follow the approved curriculum with classes like the one she has inherited:

> The attitude of the Head is appalling! He is ineffective and wet! I'm surprised the staff haven't organised a vote of no confidence! Why do staff let him get away with it? In reality, a school could not function with such a total lack of any support structure. (Joyce Carey)

She visits the teaching room of Griffith, her best friend and colleague, who immediately reads her presence as being connected to the students and counsels her not to let them get her down. She replies that this time it's not the students but the system she's about to challenge, if only she could find some Xerox paper. Her colleague replies that there is none – in fact, there are no resources at all!

Mark Green described *Dangerous Minds* as:

> All very clichéd and far too removed from reality to be taken seriously – an awful film. The portrayal of teachers like this make it appear simple and does not do us as professionals any favours as a result.

The reality of the resilient charismatic teacher film

Collectively, these films span forty years (1955-1995) and their degree of realism in the eyes of their audience is dogged by the ongoing debate about defining reality. Constrained by telling a story in 90 to 120 minutes, films cannot observe the laws of real time (Dick, 1998). When there is only a finite time available, the story must not be held up unnecessarily, and so characters' actions are subject to the rules of the *reel* world. In the words of Alfred Hitchcock: 'Cinema is life, with the boring bits cut out' (cited by Maltby and Craven, 1995: 286). There is always a gap between the *reel* and real worlds, and this is bridged by the audience accepting a representation, rather than a reproduction, of real life.

In the resilient charismatic teacher film, only the teachers who have had any experience of the real world before starting their training were able to connect with the students in a way which teachers who have not experienced other work are not – the 'born' teacher:

> Most of the heroes are outsiders who shake up the cynicism and indolence of the teaching establishment. The whole teaching profession must be remarkably dim if one simple insight by one 'new' teacher can yield such fantastic results in such a short time. (Clive Parker)

Because of the problem of real/*reel* time, this means there can often appear to be no sense of the unremitting hard work and perseverance involved in teaching. Whilst there were realistic flashes of self-doubt in some of their main characters, they appeared to spend little or no time revising their ideas about developing students' thinking. The teachers in the first sample thought that getting the real world message about teaching across via the entertainment medium of the popular film was questionable. However good a film was as a means of educating the general public about the role of a teacher, most characters and films were unrealistic and too removed from actual experience:

> One teacher manages to revolutionise the behaviour of the toughest class in the school by the application of simple common sense. During their eleven years of education this has, apparently, never been tried before. (Clive Parker)

Across the year groups, there is a diversity of relationships, but the good relationships with normal students, the inability to reach every student, the barely literate students, and the hindrance of progress through student absence are all missing in the charismatic teacher film. Examinations play a significant role in the lives of both students and teachers but, apart from *Stand and Deliver*, none were shown taking place. Joyce Carey was sceptical about the possible relationship between the real and *reel* worlds:

> The problem is, as I see it, that film makers are not interested in being realistic. They have a specific audience that they are aiming for and they need to make money. Therefore, apart from the rare exceptions, they will operate in much the same way as the tabloid press – taking the populist line and reinforcing set stereotypes (e.g. teachers must be inspirational). Film makers rarely want to make realistic films and, let's face it, who would really want to watch my average day? Six classes of kids who can barely read and write, punctuated by

mountains of paperwork and interminable meetings about the National Curriculum! Hardly stimulating viewing!

There are few restrictive measures in the *reel* world of teaching. In the real world, students would not be able to devote the time their *reel* world counterparts do to a life skills course, however relevant, in the months leading up to leaving school (*To Sir, With Love*), spend their holidays doing Mathematics (*Stand and Deliver*) or karate (*Dangerous Minds*). The external imposition of a pre-packaged curriculum has limited the creativity of teaching and learning styles. Teachers generally appear to accept the contemporary policy landscape unquestioningly, even if they know it to be wrong (Helsby, 1995). Although the government cannot directly control what happens in the classroom, the National Curriculum has made it more difficult to introduce critical approaches to pedagogy (Dale, 1989). In the real world of teaching where teachers 'deliver' a curriculum which controls them, it was refreshing to see the syllabus unfettered. But most teachers in the sample felt they had neither the ability to set their own agenda nor the room for innovation.

Reel teachers can maintain performance teaching because they do not have to endure the downside of teaching. With few exceptions, there is no administration to be dealt with, no lessons to be prepared, no work is written or marked, no tests are administered, no meetings are attended, and there is no accountability with respect to the curriculum. The charismatic teacher can give a disproportionate amount of time to the individual welfare of their students. Richard Clark said about *Dangerous Minds*:

> If this film was based on reality this teacher would be far too exhausted through prep and marking to spend so much time weeping and worrying – a fairy tale.

Teachers interact not only in the staffroom, where these films overplay the stereotypical portrayals and fail to show good relationships between teaching colleagues, but there are also meetings in departments, in faculties and in year teams. As part of a whole school team teachers liaise with and support each other constructively, and cover for absence. These films failed to portray the pace of dashing from class to class, and the varied and individual needs of students.

The charismatic teacher film does, to varying degrees, acknowledge the effect of factors beyond the classroom and the school. In the tough schools, the impoverished backgrounds of the students and the academic aspirations associated with them are all too familiar. Joyce Carey provided some examples which draw on real life:

> There are some points which strike a chord, e.g. inflexible curriculum, lack of resources, huge classes, no jobs for pupils to go to, poor backgrounds and little parental support, students having to work long hours after school, and most importantly tremendous lack of confidence and motivation in pupils when shoved into a sink group.

It is only the dedicated *reel* teachers who can be relied upon in any crisis, and the education system can be changed and overcome by an individual. In the real world, one teacher cannot turn the tide without the collective action of supportive colleagues and management:

> The idea that good/bad teachers make or break the education system is dangerous. (Are bus drivers expected to be inspirational?) Until we realize that it's the system and not the individual that's at fault, we'll never change anything. (Joyce Carey)

The popular image of teachers' work is one confined to classrooms, where teachers are judged on their performance by students, parents and Ofsted inspectors – and this is comparable to *reel* world teachers. Parents' evenings, staff meetings and marking books are invisible, just as in most charismatic teacher films. And work that extends beyond the classroom has proliferated: peer appraisal, mentoring new teachers, in-service training, and attending case meetings for individual students. Contact with parents extends beyond the annual Parents' Evening to more regular communication over increased student assessment (Hargreaves, 1994). Kirsten Scrivener provided a list of tasks she had to deal with and compared it with the work of the *reel* teacher:

> One of the key points about teaching is how teachers cope with the grind and the endless drip feed of tasks/demands – take this last couple of weeks at my school:
>
> ■ year 11 and lower 6 exam marking
> ■ year 11 reports
> ■ usual marking and preparation
> ■ year 8 Parents' Evening

- the usual crises in one's form
- the usual paperwork
- approaching meetings to prepare for, etc, etc, etc

yet still manage every now and then to have magic moments in the classroom – that's what's special about teachers and teaching.

* * *

Resilient charismatic teachers such as Richard Dadier and Mark Thackeray get their students' attention and begin the Herculean task of developing a pedagogy which is relevant to their lives. Jaime Escalante is able to uplift his students by introducing them to the mysteries of advanced mathematics, as is LouAnne Johnson with an appreciation of poetry stimulated by her Dylan/Dylan competition. Student enlightenment quickly follows, and at the end of their first year in post, the resilient charismatic teachers have accomplished their mission to rescue what are now wonderful classes of students. They have also had some success in overcoming the cynicism of colleagues. Now they have to make the all-important decision of whether to stay or leave.

But their *reel* romantic charismatic counterparts have a different fate in pleasanter surroundings. Hargreaves (1995) claims that in the traditional school, in which romantic charismatic teachers find themselves, innovative teaching is hard to pull off: 'Teachers who do not restrict their innovation (or public knowledge about it) are not tolerated and suffer the fate of Miss Jean Brodie or John Keating (in *Dead Poets Society*)' (Hargreaves, 1995: 33).

Chapter 6

I t is not only students from the inner city who are in need of an inspirational guru. In an alternative scenario in the charismatic teacher film, teachers find themselves in an educational institution which is generally unproblematic but which needs that special something only they can provide. The successful teacher is introduced into an 'impoverished environment, where 'the lovable teacher liberates his [sic] frustrated kids from the claws of an oppressive educational system' (Harry, *Guardian*, 1997a). Like their colleagues in the inner city state system, the romantic charismatic teachers also appear to live for the job and show total altruism, but more often than not they find themselves in the gentrified, fee-paying school system. The characters of Jean Brodie (*The Prime of Miss Jean Brodie*), and John Keating (*Dead Poets Society*) fall into this category. Teachers from the first sample reflect on these films.

Moving on to television, teachers from the second sample examined Simon Casey's brief career in episode one of the first series and episode eight of the second series of Channel 4's *Teachers*. Although the modern era of Jean Brodie and John Keating may initially appear to have nothing in common with the postmodern era of Simon Casey, all three charismatic teachers demonstrate elements of idealism, unorthodoxy and anarchy in their approaches.

John Keating

Although John Keating's unusual methods displease the teaching establishment and the parents, they capture the hearts and minds of many of his students: 'Now, my class, you will learn to think for yourselves again. You will learn to savour words and language. No matter what anyone tells you, words and ideas can change the world.' *Dead Poets Society* appeals to the idealistic teacher (Hammond, 1993). Phillips (1996) claims that the film had relevance for teachers and the education debate of the late 1980s. Cohen (1996: 401) called this charismatic teacher film 'arguably the most important Hollywood high school film of the 1980s'.

After the introductory lesson in the entrance hall with the photographs of the old boys of the school, the class is poised to begin studying poetry. Neil Perry is asked to read from *Understanding Poetry*, by J Evans-Pritchard. The author puts forward a model for rating poetry graphically, and as Neil reads Mr Keating translates the words into a diagram on the board. The reactions of the students vary. Some predictably look bored, whereas Richard Cameron meticulously copies the work from the board. Neil concludes his reading. Mr Keating responds to his reading with the comment, 'Excrement. That's what I think of Mr J Evans-Pritchard.' He orders the students to rip the offending pages out of their poetry books. The reaction of the student is understandable: how could a teacher ask them to deface school property? Not surprisingly, Charlie Dalton is the first to take Mr Keating at his word, and the others follow suit. Mr Keating goes out of the classroom into his office to find a suitable receptacle for the rubbish.

The noise of the pages being torn from the books apparently disturbs another member of staff, Mr McAllister, who appears in the doorway of Mr Keating's classroom and demands to know what is going on. He is flummoxed by the reappearance of Mr Keating with a waste paper basket, and makes a hasty withdrawal. Having collected up the rubbish, Mr Keating hunkers down amongst the desks and invites his students to 'huddle up'. He confides in them that they are not studying poetry because it is cute – that while he recognises that medicine, law, business and engineering are all noble pursuits and necessary to sustain life, it is poetry, beauty, romance and love that people stay alive for. It is each student's duty to contribute a verse to society: what will their verse be? Once again, the camera lingers on the face of Todd Anderson, who is enraptured by this teacher. Samantha Moore explained the desire to emulate John Keating:

Theoretically, I identify totally with the ethos of this teacher. I want to be interesting and so positive with my own classes and to give them the gift of wanting to learn. It also makes me ask whether the restrictions of the syllabi these days are trying to stifle individualism – I hope not. I particularly love this film and identify with it because the subject matter is English and more importantly, poetry. I hope that I can interest my students in poetry too.

A few months into John Keating's year at Welton, another unusual teaching style is introduced. Mr Keating stands on his desk and poses the question: Why do I stand up here? This time, when the student – Charlie Dalton again – gives the wrong answer, he taps the bell on his desk with his foot and thanks him for playing. This gets a laugh. John Keating explains that he is standing on his desk to remind himself that people must constantly look at things in a different way. He invites the boys to come and see for themselves: Charlie Dalton is one of the first up on his feet. As the boys mount the teacher's desk, John Keating encourages them to break out and find their own voice, to bring their own interpretation to what they read. They must do it now because the longer they wait the less likely they will be to find their own voice:

John Keating aims to awaken something in all pupils, to make them look at English and the world with an individualistic approach. Experience is more important than learning by rote. His aim is to make them individuals, but this style also depends on them seeing him as a leader they admire and want to follow. (Polly Ford)

The bell goes, and as the last few boys jump down from the desk, John Keating leaves the classroom, setting an additional piece of homework as he goes: each boy has to compose a poem and deliver it in front of the rest of the class on Monday. He is aware how such a leap of creativity frightens them. He emphasises this point by flashing the lights on and off at the switch by the door and intoning *The Ride of the Valkyries*. He wishes them good luck, and as a parting shot addresses the last boy left on the desk, Todd Anderson, who nearly falls off it. 'Don't you think that I don't know that this assignment scares the hell out of you, you mole!' he exclaims, and turns the lights off, leaving Todd in the dark. Sally King observed:

John Keating's underlying theme of 'Seize the Day' pervades all his teaching. He is in a very traditional school where he adopts unorthodox methods to get his ideas across, i.e. taking the students out of the classroom, tearing pages out of text books, standing on the desks. He succeeds in capturing their imaginations and making them individuals.

John Keating works in a completely different type of institution from that of the resilient charismatic teachers discussed in the previous chapter. Is his notion of pastoral care based on the development of an all-round character and the liberation of the individual spirit, or does it lead to the remaking of his students in his image? John Keating, and his principal, Mr Nolan, openly disagree about producing individuals:

> John Keating: I always thought the idea of education was to learn for yourself.
> Mr Nolan: At these boys' age? Not on your life. Tradition, John. Discipline. Prepare them for college and the rest will take care of itself.

John Keating's style of teaching is the only type worth having, yet he is out of step with his colleagues and management, which undermines those who work from other bases. According to Howard Black:

> Again we see a teacher operating a set of rules and professional values generated entirely based on their own personality. There is no sense of this teacher working as part of a team, for a common end. Indeed, there is an implication that none of the other teachers are doing their job correctly or professionally.

So long as John Keating can produce successful students, the feeling is that his unconventional methods will be tolerated. But when a problem arises his colleagues distance themselves from him. A *reel* world colleague of John Keating's is the cynic:

> George McAllister: You take a big risk by encouraging them to become artists, John. When they realise that they're not Rembrandts, Shakespeares or Mozarts, they'll hate you for it.
> John Keating: We're not talking artists, George. We're talking free thinkers.
> George McAllister: Free thinkers at 17?
> John Keating: Funny, I never pegged you as a cynic.
> George McAllister: Not a cynic, a realist.

Julian Brown observed that:

> John Keating attempts to operate in isolation from his colleagues, dealing with their bemused observation of his unorthodoxy with a

certain calm detachment. He is of course ultimately rejected by their inability to understand or accept his position.

John Keating is unprofessional in his behaviour. Dougan (1998) describes the ending to the *Dead Poets Society* story, when John Campbell, a 'radical of the highest order, a crusader of conscience' (p190) was fired from Detroit County Day School. Having seen his ex-student in the film:

> Campbell felt his former pupil had erred on the side of caution. 'Actually Robin Williams wasn't as radical a teacher as I am.' Campbell insists. 'He tells the students to rip out the pages in their books, I tell them to throw the whole thing in the garbage.' (Dougan, 1998: 207)

Having been at Detroit County Day School for almost 30 years, John Campbell was dismissed after being on disciplinary procedures because of his unorthodox methods: 'On one notable occasion he insisted that anyone could teach history. To prove his point he went out into the street, stopped the first car he found, and asked the driver to come in and take the class' (Dougan, 1998: 206). Joyce Carey wrote about John Keating:

> Again, there is the idea of the teacher having to be inspirational. We can't do that six lessons a day with classes who can't read, no learning support and a rigid and inflexible National Curriculum! Sorry!

Although the character of John Keating was based on a real teacher, Mark Green was dismissive of his abilities:

> Poetry reading in caves is not an option in Hounslow. There seems to be little of the daily grind of the teacher's day.

More than any other, this film emphasises the dichotomy between representation and reproduction of reality. It was echoed by the split in the way members of the teacher sample reacted to it. Fergus Cook reflected:

> I would like to identify with his philosophy. In an ideal world how good it would be to have the time to satisfy a passion – but it can't be done – does that sound bad? Sadly there is little room for the unorthodox in modern teaching.

Many scenes may make real world teachers catch their breath, yet they know the danger of John Keating's approach. Richard Clark commented on *Dead Poets Society*:

The film is very idealised, but at a fundamental level, it is not that different from that to which a lot of teachers aspire, e.g. raising self-esteem, self-ambition, developing individual responsibility for learning.

Despite being largely idealistic, the charismatic teacher film contains elements which teachers do aspire to. *Dead Poets Society* is a good example:

> *Dead Poets Society* is a mainstream, American film and although very enjoyable, it is romanticised, stereotypical, idealist and at times painfully corny. However, it does give a distilled, heightened, almost caricatured portrayal of how some teachers feel some of the time! (Sarah Smith)

Jean Brodie

In his biography of Maggie Smith, Coveney (1992: 126) attributed the creation of Jean Brodie as a 'subtle revenge on her Scottish puritanical mother and indeed on the Oxford High School which had, as Maggie admitted in an interview, more than a touch of the Marcia Blane'. Samantha Moore commented:

> How many teachers with the National Curriculum in one hand can spend a lesson showing the pupils their holiday slides? Or indeed how desirable is it that so much of a teacher's private life should be shared in the classroom?

There is little evidence of lesson preparation, and no student work seems to get written or marked. The syllabus is so loosely followed that Jean Brodie creates her own, being overly interested in the arts and politics and contemptuous of what the school's curriculum has to offer. Her approach would never be allowed in the current educational climate. Yet, according to Susan Greenfield (*Good Housekeeping*, November 2002): 'Every girl needs a Miss Jean Brodie to get her fired up about a subject'.

Jean Brodie is also at odds with the adults she works with in her school:

> At the Marcia Blane Academy – dedicated to maintaining the *status quo* – her methods are considered unsuitable by most of the staff. She does not develop any relationships with female members, yet flirts outrageously with the two males (Mr Lowther and Mr Lloyd).

She displays lack of respect for the senior management in front of her students. However, she loses everything: Lowther, Lloyd, her girls, her job. (Venetia Todd)

In the following scene, the tension between the headteacher, Miss McKay, and Jean Brodie is obvious. Miss McKay has questioned Miss Brodie's special set of four girls about their weekend activities with Miss Brodie, and this is why she has summoned her. Miss McKay begins with pleasantries: she thanks Miss Brodie for finding the time to see her as she knows how busy her girls keep her, and compliments her on her colourful frock. Miss Brodie claims that bright colours enliven the spirits: her credo is to 'Lift, Enliven, Stimulate'. Miss McKay is dubious whether the girls' spirits need enlivening: Marcia Blane is essentially a conservative school, which does not encourage progressive attitudes:

> Jean Brodie stands up for what she believes in when the Head attempts to get rid of her. There is a strong clash between them – does Jean Brodie encourage enrichment, or recklessness? (Sally King)

Miss McKay has noted the precocity of Miss Brodie's special girls, for which Miss Brodie thanks her. This is not the response the Headteacher expects. Miss Brodie elaborates: she is in her prime, and her girls are benefiting from this. Sensing she has the upper hand Miss Brodie gets into her stride and offers her definition of education: to lead out what is already there. While Miss McKay hopes for some putting in of information, Miss Brodie points out that this would be intrusion. Clive Parker highlighted how Jean Brodie contradicts herself:

> Superficially, pastoral care is about the development of personality and independence. The pastoral dimension seems to be at the centre of her curriculum: whatever learning of facts or skills occurs does so as an adjunct to developing an attitude of mind. In reality, however, it is about indoctrination and moulding minds in the image that she wants.

Although Miss McKay finds a discussion such as this one on education with a dedicated teacher instructive, she must move on to the main reason for summoning Miss Brodie – her weekend activities on Mr Lowther's estate with her set. Miss McKay sees it as her job to monitor the private lives of her staff both inside and outside the school walls. Miss Brodie responds, rather kindly in the circumstances, that she did not realise what a taxing load of trivia the headteacher has to concern herself with. Miss McKay replies that she has to concern herself with the Board of Governors. Miss Brodie responds that she is flattered that she is not unknown to this august group, having been at Marcia Blane six years longer than the headteacher, and having never heard anything but appreciation and approval of her teaching methods. She explains that on the Lowther estate, the woods are used for botany, and the rocks for geology, and these weekend visits are enrichment for the girls and, by extension, for Marcia Blane. Miss McKay pauses, temporarily stumped by this seemingly plausible explanation, then thanks Miss Brodie for enabling her to understand the situation better. The matter is resolved – for the time being.

Joyce Carey proposed an alternative interpretation of Jean Brodie as the romantic charismatic teacher:

> The film is clever, since it begins by setting Brodie up as someone we admire at the start – the energy, commitment and enthusiasm. We are quite likely to feel inadequate alongside this powerhouse of a woman. This is soon deflated, however, and we become aware of a sad figure, unable to take chances with her own life and instead trying to experience it through her 'girls'. We think it's about this tedious cult of the individual – the way in which special teachers can come along and inspire pupils. We feel guilty because we can't be like her. But then this concept is turned on its head since what she's opening the door to is fascism.

The teachers in the first sample are more guarded about the romantic charismatic teacher than about the resilient charismatic teacher. Although the real world teachers can appreciate why such dangerous individuals are not supported by their respective colleagues and senior managers, Richard Clark mused:

> It would be easy to say that this film is totally irrelevant, but I would like to think we carry a match to light that elusive spark that exists in most pupils. However, present trends tend to desire automatons, not creators.

After watching *The Prime of Miss Jean Brodie*, Joyce Carey wrote:

Another thing the film caused me to reflect on was Brodie's words that she gave up Teddy Lloyd 'to consecrate my life to my girls'. It's like teaching is a religious calling – a vocation, which is hogwash! The term vocation is used by the government to allow poor conditions and pay. (You wouldn't hear someone talk about consecrating their life to the role of manager of Sainsbury's, would you?!) The film reinforces the misguided stereotype of teaching as a calling/vocation.

In her reflection on the same film, Sarah Smith identified the damage done – not only to the student but also to the teacher:

This film could induce a sort of sentimental view of teaching. It arouses my concern about teachers who are *too* school-orientated: pupils go home at the end of the day, and so should we – mentally, I mean. Teachers who think school is the centre of the universe and who over-inflate their own role do not offer a balanced view to their students.

Teachers from the first sample responded thus to the six films. Both the resilient and romantic charismatic teachers who feature in them belong to the traditional form of charismatic teacher film genre. The later films *187* and *Mona Lisa Smile* (see chapter four) broke new ground. And on television, Channel 4's *Teachers* and its main character in the first two series, Simon Casey, does likewise.

Robin Williams being all inspirational in *Dead Poets Society* was one thing, ... 'Call me Simon', however, is not just unbelievable, he is unemployable too. What teacher would dare greet his class with the words 'Well, scum ...' ... . The problem with teachers who tell you to call them Simon is that being popular is more important to them than a little thing we call education. (Mourby, *Times Educational Supplement*, 08/02/02)

Simon Casey

We met Simon Casey in chapter two, where he broke into his school on his birthday, left a live sheep in one of the science labs, and stole what turns out to be Jenny's bust of Shakespeare. The tension between these two members of the English Department underpins the first episode of the first series. In the classroom, Simon's teaching and learning style is juxtaposed with Jenny's more traditional approach to studying *Romeo and Juliet*. He entertains, whereas Jenny appears to teach to the letter, and he wants to be a better teacher than Jenny in the eyes of the students. While her class merely read the text, he whips his class up into hysteria in an attempt to get his students to appreciate the passion with which the lovers want each other. Student Jeremy is the exception; he is impatient because he realises the need to pass exams, even if Simon does not. Simon encourages his students to identify what they passionately want, for example, to own Manchester United, to shag Ryan Giggs. He wants to see his students as members of his fan club – hence the fantasy sequence in which they proclaim: 'I want you to teach all of my classes', 'I want you to be Headmaster', 'I want to be *you*, Simon.' As they chant 'Simon! Simon!', Jenny enters and interrupts with a sarcastic put down: 'Make some more noise ... my class is finding it too easy to concentrate.' On her icy departure his students reassure him: 'Don't worry, Simon, she talks to us like that too.'

Simon is a maverick. He has energy and passion, he wants to stimulate and engage his students and for learning to be fun. As Fiona McIntyre reflected:

> Having a good relationship with your students (being able to joke and laugh with them) can be equally as motivating as shouting. Within limits!

His style is liberal, informal and relaxed – perhaps this is preferable to sticking rigidly to pre-prepared lesson plans that have to be delivered:

> I think the best teaching is risky, lively and a little risqué – so some of Simon's style was positive for me – it was suggested however, that if a teacher is like that then he/she must be lacking something of professionalism. (Peter Taylor)

Whilst Simon encourages them to understand historical texts in a contemporary light, he talks at them rather than with them, adapting their comments to make them fit with his own pre-conceived ideas. He relies on instant inspiration, which demonstrates a lack of preparation, and this results in unsuitable responses from his students.

His private war with Jenny over teaching and learning styles extends to their differences on issues of pastoral care. As tutor and acting year head to the boy who attempts to tattoo himself in the boys' toilets, Simon should report the matter to Jenny. But Simon wants to be the students' friend, to be on their side and gain their trust. He does not appreciate his wider pastoral responsibility, and that he is legally obliged to report dangerous activities such as tattooing and ear-piercing to a higher authority. He does not want to boss the students around, so in order to avoid disciplining students he does not uphold the school rules. This evokes the comment:

> My headteacher once said, as a member of this school you *must* abide by the rules and reinforce them whether you like them or not. If you do not agree with this you don't have anything to do here. (Barbara Miles)

Simon presents a public image that he puts the students' needs first and appears to care, albeit irresponsibly, but in private he declares the opposite. Simon and his friends congregate in the pub every night after school, and collegial support is cloaked in juvenile behaviour such as excessive swearing, drinking and smoking and childish, laddish and disrespectful banter. Charlotte Hope notes:

> His closest colleagues don't support him and joke about his lack of marking and his professional conduct, and join in his pranks. They are depicted as irresponsible adults unable to separate fun and enjoyment from work.

There is no distinction between being in school and being out of school:

> Support is via socialising rather than on a professional basis, but that kind of support is clearly very important. I know from conversations with people in their early/mid twenties that this portrayal made teaching seem far more attractive. (Sarah Smith)

However, Zuleika Knight commented:

> I wish! He is all fun loving and carefree. There is no real mention of the stresses and strains of the profession. I'm not sure I could handle the eternal hangover.

Back in school, Simon dodges all departmental responsibilities: he fails to meet deadlines and is blissfully unaware of the escalating problems this causes Bob, his Head of Department. But Bob does not explore why there is a problem, though as Head of Department, he should. There is no teamwork, except when Simon can longer avoid the demands of his Head of Department or his students, who have been asking for their essays back, and he offers his colleagues a half pint per essay if they will help him with his marking:

> Professionally, he is basically an egocentric loner. Ironically, the only scene of collegiate action represents a betrayal of the students: he persuades his colleagues to mark his [students'] essays collectively in the pub. His colleagues are either represented as admiring or at worst mildly critical of his attitude, for example, Jenny: 'It's not supposed to be entertainment.' (Julian Brown)

When their private war erupts in a public outburst, the headteacher reprimands Simon and Jenny. Simon does not want to be a 'teaching machine', and an approach such as his headteacher's does need challenging because she is dangerous:

> He was pressured by the culture of the school, one that is currently prevalent in education that seems to want to promote a specific view of what professionalism means. It is a dominant cultural view that creates in teachers like Simon a fear of freedom, isolation and pressure to conform, which is what he does ... It was good to see him come to his senses though ... (Peter Taylor)

As we shall see, Joyce Carey's comment about Simon proves to be prophetic:

> There's a sense that he's playing at being a teacher. Like so many now, he'll stick at it for a couple of years and move on. He'll be young enough to and it's unlikely there will be many incentives for him to stay.

By the second series, Simon and Jenny have buried their differences, and she has become part of the pub-going crowd, when her private life allows her to. There was general agreement amongst the second teacher sample that Simon is doing better, although there is still plenty of room for improvement. He is calmer, more controlled, more formal, yet he retains his cynicism and still tries to be trendy. He is now anxious to be seen to be doing the right thing. The students are more involved, better behaved, more willing to listen, and engaged in a more positive and focused way:

> Simon is trying to be more formal but he is still trying to be relevant and sees himself as a maverick not bound by rules. If I were his pupil I'd feel very frustrated. (Lucinda Baker)

Simon shows that he is now willing to discipline poor behaviour, confiscating one of the ubiquitous mobile phones. He cannot resist looking through the student's list of phone numbers, and the breadth of her social circle at such a young age makes him feel that life is somehow passing him by. Having set his class a task entitled My Week and observing how they quickly settle down and start writing, Simon decides to try the activity for himself. Unfortunately, he cannot think of a thing to write, and this reinforces his desire to do something with his life before it is too late. Things must be serious – he has begun to question the point of the nightly excursion to the pub!

Simon still doesn't know whether he wants to be a teacher, so Susan, on whom he relies, suggests some time out. Having bought an airline ticket for South America and then found out he can't get a refund, he is forced to go and see the headteacher and resign immediately.

> Simon's plea 'Can't I just run away?' will ring a bell with many teachers, I'm sure. He's been in post for a year and yet is already facing burn-out. Many of his colleagues are young, yet are facing the same problem. It seems that if Simon is to stay he must conform. He cannot, so he goes. Is this his fault or the system's? (Joyce Carey)

The reaction of the headteacher is predictable: bad language aside, she calls him disruptive and irresponsible and tells him he is finished for good in teaching. Simon's plea that he cannot stay in the school any longer and that he has to take this action before he dies understandably falls on deaf ears. He ignores the headteacher's advice that it will be difficult to get another job because he has broken his contract, reinforcing his unreliability and lack of professionalism.

When handing in his notice, he does not think about the stability of his tutor group or his teaching groups. He tells his students that they deserve a good teacher, although he admits he is not quite sure how another teacher will be found for them. The students react by winding him up with fake tears, which further enhances his cynicism.

> His decision to leave without working out his notice is characteristically irresponsible. He gives no thought to how this dumps on both his classes and his colleagues. (Julian Brown)

Given that he also drops his colleagues in it, their reaction is decent and, despite his protest that he does not want a celebration to mark his imminent departure, they organise a staff leaving party.

122 • CARRY ON, TEACHERS!

The television series *Teachers* perhaps suggests that the end is in sight for the charismatic teachers that have featured in films and television programmes for so long. Stereotyping exaggerates and fixes the essential characteristics of members of a group to such a degree that a stereotype of a stereotype can develop (Perkins, cited by Lacey, 1998). Samantha Moore reflected:

> Initially it would be easy to say that this representation is a long way from reality – but on reflection I feel that he is a caricature of many different aspects that are pervading teaching and changes in attitudes that are to be found in the real world. Possibly teaching is no longer seen as a calling but a job that people can do and acknowledge no responsibility for their wider influence on the lives of others.

The idea of teaching as a sacred profession was similarly challenged by Sarah Smith:

> The fashion/mood of the moment is to be cynical, throwaway – the non-martyr approach, the fallibility of the characters. Perhaps the public's perception could in some ways benefit from a less sanctimonious image?

Charlotte Hope emphasised how the errors and bad behaviour of the *reel* teachers are an important part of the humour of the series:

> Teaching is now more businesslike – schools have a corporate vision and staff need to buy into this or the school won't function effectively. *Teachers* uses current issues, highlights and ridicules them – that's part of the appeal.

Of course, such a comedic image can further undermine the prevailing view of a profession already under siege. Lucinda Baker observed:

> Whoever wrote it must think that teachers swearing, getting pissed and having sex is funny – it isn't! They are just people after all – it's only pupils who think we don't have lives out of school.

Laura Cross spoke for the majority of the teachers in the second sample when she said:

> The level of unprofessionalism displayed is alarming and damaging to the profession.

Simon Casey's carefree approach is not normal teacher conduct for the twentieth-first century. As Julian Brown commented:

If I'm overly critical of Simon, it's probably because I *was* Simon back in the seventies! But that was a different time. I find it hard to see how someone like that could survive in the present teaching climate – which is probably why Simon doesn't. It was a shame that a correlation was implied between an intuitive teacher, able to relate and talk in a relaxed way with his students, and the feckless irresponsible egotist represented here.

Peter Taylor concurred:

> In some ways I think I am very much like Simon – certainly in terms of style, questioning, fun, etc. I am much more conscientious in terms of colleagues though. I value teamwork very highly. I hate prescriptive initiatives! I am much more conscientious in terms of assessment of students' work too.

Simon Casey is faced with the dilemma that all teachers have had. He wants to be himself, a person first and foremost, but how does staying true to that person correlate with the needs of his students? It takes time to find an approach in the classroom which works for both teacher and students. Simon gives himself just over a year, and his sudden departure in the second series caused Miriam Harris to reflect on how much the individual teacher matters to the system:

> How important can a teacher be? Sometimes there is a feeling that schools evolve and change and you have a relatively small impact on schools and students, even though you put a great amount of effort into your teaching.

Peter Taylor raised the key issue about a system which takes and takes without putting something back:

> It really makes me think about my own position as a teacher, and whether I want to continue to do it. I am committed and fervent about education, but it has to be for liberation and to create a critical consciousness in those I teach. In the current climate with such a lack of control over curriculum content, assessment, new prescriptive initiatives, league tables, jumping through hoops to get paid, Poitier's exercises in professional development, Ofsted, non-qualified staff teaching lessons, the obsession with discipline etc, etc, etc, etc, etc ... I am seriously considering getting out! But maybe I'm being too cynical to think that things won't improve?

But just *how* important is the school setting to the lives of these twenty-something members of Generation X, with their work values of loyalty to self and lifestyle, the 'greed is good' generation alluded to in chapter three? As Mary Price commented:

> It's a witty, fast-paced, cool programme but it's not really about teaching. Students and learning are incidental – this could be set in an office selling prosthetics!

Peter Taylor agreed:

> I thought in the first two episodes the notion of 'Teachers' was incidental really to the stories of the main character and his relationships with several of the other. It could just as easily have been called 'Doctors', 'Road-Sweepers', 'Cricketers', etc.

Lucinda Baker felt that *Teachers* was 'a missed opportunity':

> The programme doesn't really raise any questions for me about contemporary teaching as the children aren't real. There are no behavioural problems, horrible kids, issues about resources, money, marking, arguments about setting, lost video cassettes, tedious invigilations – the whole, brilliant, wonderful, intense, fascinating world of a secondary school!

* * *

There are too many constraints for the students to be the free thinkers John Keating and Jean Brodie want them to be, and their romantic and revolutionary ideologies hardly echo either their schools' or the parents' aims. Jean Brodie has little affection for the official curriculum, which lacks the elements of classical beauty which interest her, and where the exploration of feelings and development of personality are as important as the accruing of factual knowledge. Aloof, misinformed and antagonistic, she regards most of her colleagues with contempt. Whilst Jean Brodie is initially able to win her argument for her unorthodox and progressive teaching methods with the governors she, like John Keating, finally has to leave the school.

The romantic charismatic teacher film is salutary in that it reminds teachers that they do or can have more influence over some students than they realise and that can help to make the job more gratifying. Teachers have the power to be inspirational. They can be role models to the benefit – or detriment – of certain students.

In *Teachers*, Simon Casey is a detrimental role model. The series identifies issues real world teachers are familiar with: in ridiculing them, there is the opportunity to step back and laugh at ourselves. But Mary Price questioned this attitude:

> I think that most teachers are very committed to their profession and to their students. Yes, it must be very difficult in schools where students are wholly resistant to education and yes, our lives are made difficult by those in authority and by Government edicts. But can a show like this be truly seen as a means of resistance? Should we all become beer-swilling, hung over, bitchy, lazy, unfocused, unprofessional louts to evade difficult students and demanding authority?

Clinical psychologist Oliver James describes *Teachers* as a kind of *samizdat* literature (Bunting, *TES Jobs*, 31/05/02). If the teaching profession continues on its current course, then he advises real world teachers adopting their *reel* world counterparts' approach: 'you can try within a totalitarian system to playfully live within it, to keep a sense of yourself, and then maybe you can give something extra to the children'. Thus, 'a series that has deliberately tried to avoid being didactic has ended up with a little something to teach' (Buss, *TES Friday*, 16/03/01).

Conclusion

McCulloch and Richardson (2000) stress the importance of utilising visual sources in the study of individuals, institutions and social policies. They observe that as well as fictional and factual programmes on British television, 'the British cinema has been no less fertile as a potential source of visual evidence' (p110). In mapping important aspects of macro and micro professional change, films provide historical documentation of the teaching culture of which current members of the profession are the descendants. In attempting to establish a real/*reel* overlap, what can members of my teacher samples take away from their examples from screen culture? Julian Brown provides a useful summary of his *reel* world counterparts in charismatic teacher films:

> I have come to the conclusion that all the films are basically from the same mould and contain the same assumptions. Effective teachers are charismatic. When these main characters have had experience of the real world (as a marine or engineer), they are able to connect with students in a way that a conventional teacher cannot. They are invariably out of step with colleagues, the management of the school and the educational establishment, which are usually represented as ineffective, moribund or downright malicious – certainly out of touch with students. They succeed without reference to any support from the school system.

These Messiah-like individuals are able, mainly by the force of personality, to change depressing and failing systems by turning students around and tackling the apathy of colleagues. Such messages do practising teachers a disservice, as these prevailing images can only lead to disappointment. Teachers cannot inspire every lesson of every day of every academic year.

These films don't reflect the mundane aspects of teaching but this is inevitable given the genre. Teaching is often about endurance, stamina, perseverance, coping with daily minutiae and not about all-singing, all-dancing lessons every time! (Kirsten Scrivener)

Although *Blackboard Jungle* begins by asserting that the problems in schools have their origins outside the classroom, failing education continues to be laid at the door of teachers. Should charisma take the place of everything else?

The issue of charisma is very real. There is no questioning its value as an extrinsic device in motivating students. As a drama teacher, I've thought a lot about this. However, it is evident that charisma on its own is not enough and, when used in a self-promoting manner, can be potentially damaging. (Julian Brown)

Real world teachers have experienced what their *reel* world counterparts have not: diminished creativity, and the reduction of their work to technician status thanks to the National Curriculum which has imposed models of teaching via teacher-proof curriculum programmes and standardised tests. The apparent simplicity of the teaching task is underpinned by individuals who can set their own agenda with the one class they are responsible for, and can overcome their problems, and the attitude of cynical colleagues, with their innate inspiration. The work in the classroom featured in the charismatic teacher film is just the tip of the iceberg when it comes to the professional life of the real world teacher.

The working hours (contact hours) of a teacher discriminate against a full commitment to every lesson, every day, every week of every term. But society tends to get what it pays for. I personally think society (or the government) gets more than it pays for from most teachers. (Richard Clark)

These films do not show the time spent by teachers outside the hours of nine to three thirty, where their workload takes up time not only after six and at weekends but also during the seemingly long holidays. They lack any perception of the work involved in contemporary teaching. Clive Parker makes this clear:

The constant, energy-sapping work which is needed to make even small amounts of progress with difficult students. There isn't a magic

CARRY ON, TEACHERS! • 129

key that will instantly turn them around. The sense of the school as a whole establishment working together (for the most part). Most of these teachers only seem to have one class. Where is the sense that they have too many plates to spin to devote all the energy and attention they would like to particular groups?

In addition to their role as subject teachers, and the pastoral care implicit in their interactions with students, teachers have responsibilities as tutors. They deal with disciplinary matters in their own tutor group when they occur, although the level of interaction will vary with individual teachers and how they rank pastoral care. In the current educational climate, what is now known as students' spiritual and moral welfare is a specific focus of school inspections, and under the 1988 Education Reform Act, teachers have responsibility for these dimensions of student experience (Capel *et al*, 1995). But it is arguably more difficult to encourage the values which underlie this area of experience in a contemporary culture which emphasises the rights of the self above anyone else's. Thanks to the subject-specific nature of the National Curriculum, the amount and quality of pastoral care found in schools has decreased (Murray, 1995). Polly Ford reflected:

> The films made me question my adherence to the academic aspects of course content. They made me think that I should get back to knowing more about the backgrounds of pupils, which used to be a priority but has gone by the wayside.

Mary Price alluded to the well-known saying in initial teacher training circles: teachers are teachers firstly of children, secondly of subjects:

> In a lot of these kinds of movies, the teachers are often more concerned about relationships with students than teaching a subject. In my school life, it's more about getting my subject across – is this right? What is education about?

The idea that students respond to positive encouragement is underpinned by mutual respect between teacher and student:

> Although the key features of *To Sir, With Love* involved cliché and much stereotyping, and although the transformation of Sir's class was deeply unconvincing, there was a fundamental truth at work: a teacher and pupil can only progress on the basis of mutual respect. I sometimes need to be reminded of this! (Julian Brown)

Katherine Fox commented on Jaime Escalante's rapport with his students:

> He never argued with pupils in a confrontational way. He never moved from his stance. They either learned, and worked his way or went away – and the whole class backed him. There is a lot here I need to think about using.

Teaching is not made for the purpose of generating exciting cinema, and perhaps the predominance of American films in the film sample seen by the first group of teachers indicates that British film makers realise that there is little dramatic interest in the average teachers, students and school, unless one imposes a grossly unacceptable distortion of teaching.

> It raises more questions, in fact I think all of the films do, about the validity of films which fail to portray our profession in anything like a real manner. It is sad that the only teacher considered worth portraying is the maverick loner, bucking an uncaring and ineffective system. But then, who'd watch them? Who would watch the truth – no dramatic interest at all. (Laura Cross)

Clive Parker puts his finger on the problem:

> When will somebody make a film that suggests that the majority of teachers are doing all they can and that the solution to any problems lies in a concerted effort between schools/parents/society/employers? Where is the film that throws down the gauntlet to people and agencies outside the school to make more effort?

Film is a poor medium through which to portray the work of a teacher. Because a large constituent of the job is uncinematic – the bureaucracy of paperwork, lesson preparation, marking and meetings – this inevitably results in stereotypical and sensational representations.

> I think these films have to be seen for what they are – fiction. Obviously, there is a level at which their messages will be absorbed, albeit subconsciously. However, anyone who goes into teaching because they loved *Dead Poets* (or the medical profession because of *Casualty* come to that) really must be a little lacking somewhere. (Joyce Carey)

There is no escape from charismatic teachers who altruistically dedicate their lives to their work to the exclusion of all else, and such portrayals evoke a degree of negativity in the responses of real world teachers. However, it is important to situate that negativity within their own experiences, within the decline in the autonomy and collegiality of teachers, centralised control of curriculum and associated practices (see Tomlinson 2001 among others). Despite their real world experience, responses to the charismatic teacher film *do* demonstrate that teachers can find elements of overlap between the real and the *reel* which cause them to reflect on their everyday practices.

As in real life, moments of doubt and anxiety are shown before the character enters the unruly classroom for the first time. It is up to teachers to find the coping strategies and establish the classroom ground rules which work for them. Once inside the classroom, the personality of the teacher develops: inspiration, warmth, fairness, sense of humour, self-reliance and perseverance. Charismatic teachers must have some depth to their characters and their behaviour must connect with examples from the everyday world, although combining entertainment with education will mean some simplification of problems. Nevertheless, screen culture describes recognisable everyday situations in their narratives and thus establishes a point of contact between the *reel* world and the real experience of its audience.

> In some ways I think that *Teachers* reflects the very changing culture that we now live in where teachers are treated with disdain – expected to entertain, swear and be part of the culture of young people rather than an example, a figure to respect. In other ways I feel that the series is trying to demystify the role of teaching and say that we are ordinary people, doing a thankless job rather than saints who should be better than other people. (Samantha Moore)

The real/*reel* worlds overlap when teachers can identify elements of their everyday lives – albeit idealistically portrayed – in the charismatic teacher film, and can reflect on how to practically accommodate such aspects within their individual work context:

> Teachers are under too many constraints to be such free spirits, *although* what the films concentrate and intensify in terms of the excitement of good chemistry with a class or individual is also a real reflection of teaching. (Kirsten Scrivener)

Although teachers may dispute that their charismatic *reel* world counterparts impact on the real world of teaching, particularly in light of their own experiences, screen culture has potential for influence. The popular culture audience is often stereotyped as being sick, drugged, and passively accepting of a diet of trivia, but popular film demands to be examined precisely because it is a source of significance and pleasure for so many people, including members of the teaching profession. I cannot be alone in feeling 'the powerful draw of a mid-afternoon black-and-white film' (Williams, *Guardian Weekend*, 15/02/03). This is where, as Crook (1999: 365) rejoices: 'images of the educational past are frequently to be seen on the small screen. Tucked away in the afternoon matinee schedules it is not uncommon to find such films as *Goodbye Mr Chips, The Browning Version* or *The Prime of Miss Jean Brodie.*' In 2004, ITV1's Christmas Day afternoon schedule contained a repeat of *Goodbye Mr Chips*, starring Martin Clunes and on New Year's Day, Stephen Fry starred in *Tom Brown's Schooldays.*

Interestingly, the charismatic teacher film remains popular with leading Hollywood stars, who seem happy to include a movie of this category in their portfolio of performances, for example, Sidney Poitier in *To Sir, With Love*, Robin Williams in *Dead Poets Society*, Michelle Pfeiffer in *Dangerous Minds* and Julia Roberts in *Mona Lisa Smile*. Starring in a charismatic teacher film has won Oscars for Robert Donat in *Goodbye, Mr. Chips* – who beat off competition from the likes of Clark Gable and Laurence Olivier in 1939 – and Maggie Smith in *The Prime of Miss Jean Brodie.*

The innovation of the teaching 'Oscars' in 1999 reinforces the real/*reel* overlap between the two worlds of screen and teaching culture. On the third awards evening in 2001, one teacher was heard to remark that teaching was akin to six matinee performances a day (Woodward, *Guardian Education*, 06/11/01). Philip Beadle, the winner of the Best Teacher in a Secondary School 'Oscar' in 2004, claimed that his wife described him as 'a children's entertainer' (The Teaching Awards, 24/10/04). In the same vein, according to Wragg and Wood (1994), teachers have likened the start of a new term to a first night performance: 'If you are teaching a class or lecturing to an audience you have also, in some important senses, to perform – to use the tricks and techniques of an actor' (Richardson, 2002: viii).

And now other people are getting in on the act. Former cabinet minister Clare Short took part in a BBC documentary in which she worked as a teacher at Southfields Community College in South London for a week. She thought 'it might make people think about teachers' (Barber, *Observer*, 22/02/04). One of the students she taught said that she told one class the same story three times, and that much of the lesson content was irrelevant. The headteacher was not impressed with Ms Short's timekeeping; one morning she managed to arrive only five minutes before the 8.20 a.m. start because she couldn't find her hairdryer (Bloom, *Times Educational Supplement*, 27/02/04). But the teacher Ms Short took over from, Celina Viner, found that the experience made her realise how much she loved being a teacher (Viner, Guardian Education, 17/02/04). Ms Short's experience was less positive: 'I was ridiculous to do it' (Barber, *Observer*, 22/02/04). *So You Think You Can Teach?*, a Channel 5 production, features celebrities Janet Street-Porter, Shaun Williamson and Tamara Beckwith in the classroom (Barnes, *Independent on Sunday*, 26/12/04).

Later on this year, I shall be sitting in the National Theatre on a spring afternoon watching *The History Boys*, the success of which rivals *The Madness of George III*, *Amadeus* and *Racing Demon* (Jury, *Independent*, 08/09/04). Together with the aforementioned ITV1 drama *Ahead of the Class*, featuring Julie Walters as Marie Stubbs, these productions imply that the mandatory nature of schooling potentially provides a never-ending source of stories, and whilst recognised genres such as the western are no longer popular, 'the teacher film refuses to die' (Landesman, *Sunday Times*, 12/05/96).

Who needs a Teachers TV channel with its tips on behaviour management, fly-on-the-classroom-wall programmes about gifted teachers, and classroom makeovers (Shaw, *Times Educational Supplement*, 13/02/04; Ward, *Guardian*, 25/11/04), when from *Blackboard Jungle* to *Mona Lisa Smile* there is an endless and enjoyable supply of screen culture representations of teachers? In an age when the visual is pre-eminent, charismatic teacher films and television series will arguably have an increasing – and enduring – influence on successive generations of teachers.

References

Aldgate A (1995) *Censorship in the Permissive Society: British Cinema and Theatre 1955-1965*. Oxford: Clarendon Press

Aldgate A and Richards J (1999) (new edition) *Best of British: Cinema and Society from 1930 to the Present*. London: I B Tauris and Co

Aldrich R (1996) *Education for the Nation*. London: Cassell

Alexander R J (1984) Innovation and Continuity in the Initial Teacher Education Curriculum, in R J Alexander, M Craft and J Lynch (eds) *Change in Teacher Education: Context and Provision Since Robbins*. London: Holt Rinehart Winston

Andrew D (1998) Film and History, in J Hill and P Church Gibson (eds) *The Oxford Guide to Film Studies*. Oxford: Oxford University Press

Asthana A and Townsend M (2004) Teaching becomes class act at last, *Observer*, 11 April

Avis J (1991) The strange fate of progressive education, in Education Group II, Department of Cultural Studies, University of Birmingham *Education Limited: Schooling, training and the New Right in England since 1979*. London: Unwin Hyman

Ayers W A (2001) Teacher Ain't Nothin' but a Hero: Teachers and Teaching in Film, in P Joseph Bolotin and G E Burnaford (eds) (2nd edition) *Images of Schoolteachers in America*. London: Lawrence Erlbaum Associates

Bailey B (2000) The Impact of Mandated Change on Teachers, in N Bascia and A Hargreaves (eds) *The Sharp Edge of Educational Change: Teaching, leading and the realities of reform*. London: Routledge/Falmer

Baker M (1994) *Who Rules Our Schools?* London: Hodder and Stoughton

Baker M (2000a) Speak up, Sir! *Guardian*, 13 June

Baker M (2000b) Does education get the media it deserves? An Inaugural Lecture, Institute of Education, University of London

Baker M (2001) Smile through the pain because you love it, *Times Educational Supplement*, 11 May

Ball S J (1999) Myth: Good Management Makes Good Schools, in B O'Hagan (ed) *Modern Educational myths: The future of democratic comprehensive education*. London: Kogan Page

Barber L (2004) That'll teach her ... , *Observer*, 22 February

Barnes A (2004) Nearly 200 reality TV shows set for 2005, *Independent on Sunday*, 26 December

Barnes J (1999) But, minister ..., *Times Educational Supplement*, 2 April

Blackburn K (1975) *The Tutor.* London: Heinemann Organization in Schools series

Bloom A (2004) Can't teach, won't listen, *Times Educational Supplement*, 27 February

Bloom A (2004) Lock up your pupils, *Times Educational Supplement*, 25 June

Bodnar S J (1996) Masculinity in the Classroom: Toward an Understanding of Male Secondary Teachers in Hollywood Films (Men Teachers), Wayne State University (EdD)

Bradshaw N (1997) Class war, *Time Out*, 10-17 September: 20

Bradshaw P (2004) Mona Lisa Smile, *Guardian*, 5 March

Bright M and Ross R (2000) *Mr Carry On: The Life and Work of Peter Rogers.* London: BBC Worldwide

Broadcast, 9 July, 1999: 3

Brown R (1999) TV offers teachers its reflected glory, *Times Educational Supplement*, 9 April

Bryanston Newsletter, 4 May, 1961

Bunting C (2002) On yer bike, *TES Jobs*, 31 May

Burgess R (1984) Headship: Freedom or Constraint, in S J Ball (ed) *Comprehensive Schooling: A Reader.* London: Falmer Press

Buss R (1988) Class acting, *Times Educational Supplement*, 2 December

Buss R (1996) A dangerous load of popcorn, *Times Educational Supplement*, 26 January

Buss R (1996) If not, you can always teach ... , *Times Educational Supplement*, 24 May

Buss R (2000) TV, *TES Friday*, 23 June

Buss R (2001) TV, *TES Friday*, 16 March

Calderhead J and Shorrock S B (1997) *Understanding Teacher Education: Case Studies in the Professional Development of Beginning Teachers.* London: Falmer Press

Cameron I, Shivas M, Mayersburg P and Perkins V F (1965) Interviews with Richard Brooks, transcribed from tape-recorded interviews, and corrected afterwards, *Movie*, number 12, April: 2-9

Capel S, Leask M and Turner T (1995) *Learning to Teach in the Secondary School: A Companion to School Experience.* London: Routledge

Carlyle D and Woods P (2002) *Emotions of Teacher Stress.* Stoke on Trent: Trentham Books

Carvel J (1997) Picking a fight in the classroom, *Guardian*, 5 February

Carvel J (1999) Surge in teachers wanting jobs abroad, says VSO, *Guardian*, 25 February

Carvel J (1999) Teachers to shun payment by results, *Guardian*, 13 October

Carvel J (2000) Teachers reject performance pay boycott, *Guardian*, 18 February

Chitty C and Dunford J (eds) (1999) *State Schools: New Labour and the Conservative Legacy.* London: Woburn Press

Chumo II P N (1996) *Films in Review*, 47 (5/6): 63-64

Clemett A J and Pearce J S (1986) *The Evaluation of Pastoral Care.* Oxford: Basil Blackwell

Cohen S (1996) Postmodernity, The New Cultural History, Film: Resistant Images of Education, *Paedagogica Historica*, volume XXXII: 395-420

Cole M (1985) 'The Tender Trap'? Commitment and Consciousness in Entrants to Teaching, in S J Ball and I F Goodson (eds) *Teachers' Lives and Careers*. London: Falmer Press

Cornwell T (1996) Tear-jerker touches a chord, *Times Educational Supplement*, 10 May

Coveney M (1992) *Maggie Smith: A Bright Particular Star*. London: Victor Gollancz

Crace J (1999) Why teachers don't want a Swedish lesson, *Guardian Jobs and Money*, 8 May

Crace J (2001) Reality television, *Guardian Education*, 27 March

Croft M (1961) Saga of Censorship, *Observer*, 4 June

Crook D (1999) Viewing the past: the treatment of history of education on British television since 1985, *History of Education*, 28 (3): 365-369

Cross A (1988) *Cineaste*, 16 (4): 52-54

Crossley N (2004) Pick of the day, *G2*, 26 October

Dale R (1989) The State and Education Policy. Milton Keynes: Open University Press

Dalton M (1999) *The Hollywood Curriculum: Teachers and Teaching in the Movies*. New York: Peter Lang

Day C (2000) Teachers in the Twenty-first Century: time to renew the vision [1], *Teachers and Teaching*, 6 (1): 101-115

Dean C, Barnard N and Henry J (2000) Teachers flocking to cross threshold, *Times Educational Supplement*, 16 June

'Dear Mr Blunkett ...' *Times Educational Supplement*, 6 November, 1998

Department of Education and Science and the Welsh Office (1989) *Discipline in Schools. Report of the Committee of Enquiry Chaired by Lord Elton (The Elton Report)*. London: HMSO

Department for Education and Employment (1998) (Summary) *Teachers meeting the challenge of change*. London: DfEE

Desforges C (1995) Teaching for Order and Control, in C Desforges (ed) *An Introduction to Teaching: Psychological Perspectives*. Oxford: Blackwell

Devrell S (1999) Strokes, mass hysteria – it must be Ofsted Day, *Independent Education*, 6 May

Dick B F (1998) (third edition) *Anatomy of Film*. New York: St Martin's Press

Dickinson K (2000) *Sight and Sound*, 10 (2): 49-50

Dodd C (1999) Lessons in life, *Radio Times*, 19-25 June

Dougan A (1998) *Robin Williams*. London: Orion

Dougherty R (1997) 187, *Sight and Sound*, 7 (9): 52-53

Duncan P (1996) Interview with Bill Buchanan, *Creative Screenwriting*, Summer: 37-40

Dunford J E (1998) *Her Majesty's Inspectorate Since 1944: Standard Bearers or Turbulent Priests*. London: Woburn Press

Dyer G (1982) *Advertising As Communication*. London: Routledge

Edwards M (1999) 'Myth' of teaching as a vocation, *Times Educational Supplement*, 19 November

Elliott L (1999) Teachers are Britain's unhappiest workers, *Guardian*, 13 March

Else M (2001) Draw on talented underclass, *Times Educational Supplement*, 3 August

Farber P and Holm G (1994) A Brotherhood of Heroes: The Charismatic Educator in Recent American Movies, in P Farber, E Provenzo Jr and G Holm (eds) *Schooling in the Light of Popular Culture*. Albany NJ: SUNY Press

Farber P, Provenzo E Jr and Holm G (eds) (1994) *Schooling in the Light of Popular Culture*. Albany NJ: SUNY Press

'Festival Head's Offer To Resign', *Daily Telegraph*, 1 September, 1955

Fitzsimmons C (2001) I Quit, *Guardian*, 9 January

Ford M (2003) Let that be a lesson, *Big Issue*, 4-10 August

Fountain N and Ahuja A (1994) The tale of Haley the Comet, *Guardian* 2, 12 April

Francis P (2001) *The Best Policy? Honesty in education, 1997-2001*. Shropshire: Liberty Books

Francke L (1996) *Sight and Sound*, 6 (1), January: 37

Fullan M and Hargreaves A (1992) *What's Worth Fighting For In Your School? Working together for improvement*. Buckingham: Open University Press

Furlong J (2001) Reforming teacher education, reforming teaching: accountability, professionalism and competence, in R Phillips and J Furlong (eds) *Education, Reform and the State: 25 years of politics, policy and practice*. London: Routledge/Falmer

Garner R (2002) An inspector calls it time, *Independent Education*, 25 April

Gehring W D (1988) Parody, in W D Gehring (ed) *Handbook of American Film Genres*. London: Greenwood Press

Gilbey R (1997) Some people never learn, *Independent*, 11 September

Giroux H (1993) Reclaiming the Social: Pedagogy, Resistance, and Politics in Celluloid Culture, in J Collins, H Radner and A P Collins (eds) *Film Theory Goes To The Movies*. London: Routledge

Giroux H (1997) Is There a Place for Cultural Studies in Colleges of Education? In H Giroux (ed) with P Shannon *Education and Cultural Studies: Toward a Performative Practice*. London: Routledge

Giroux H (2002) *Breaking in to the Movies*. Oxford: Blackwell Publishers

Glancy H M (1999) *When Hollywood Loved Britain: The Hollywood 'British' Film, 1939-45*. Manchester: Manchester University Press

Goodlad J I (1990) The Occupation of Teaching in Schools, in J I Goodlad, R Soder and K A Sirotnik (eds) *The Moral Dimensions of Teaching*. Oxford: Jossey-Bass Publishers

Grayling A C (2001) The last word, *Guardian*, 1 September

Greenfield S (2002) How to make science sexy for our daughters, *Good Housekeeping*, November

Hamblin D (1978) *The Teacher and Pastoral Care*. Oxford: Blackwell

Hammond M (1993) The Historical and Hysterical: Melodrama, War and Masculinity in Dead Poets Society, in P Kirkham and J Thumim (eds) *You Tarzan: Masculinity, Movies and Men*. London: Lawrence and Wishart

Handler Spitz E (1992) CARPE DIEM, CARPE MORTEM: Reflections on Dead Poets Society, *Post Script*, 11 (3), Summer: 19-31

Hargreaves A (1984) Experience counts, theory doesn't: how teachers talk about their work, *Sociology of Education*, volume 56, October: 244-254

Hargreaves A (1994) *Changing Teachers, Changing Times: Teachers' Work and Culture in the Postmodern Age*. London: Cassell

Hargreaves A (1996) Cultures of teaching, in A Pollard (ed) *Readings for Reflective Teaching in the Primary School*. London: Cassell

Hargreaves A (2000) Four Ages of Professionalism and Professional Learning, *Teachers and Teaching: Theory and Practice*, 6 (2): 151-178

Hargreaves A and Lo L N K (2000) The Paradoxical Profession: Teaching at the Turn of the Century, *Prospects*, xxx (2), June: 167-180

Hargreaves D H (1982) *The challenge for the comprehensive school: Culture, curriculum and community*. London: Routledge and Kegan Paul

Hargreaves D H (1995) School Culture, School Effectiveness and School Improvement, *School Effectiveness and School Improvement*, 6 (1): 23-46

Harry A (1997a) You at the back – how do school movies reflect the culture of today? *Guardian*, 12 September

Harry A (1997b) To Sir, with a knife, *Black Film Bulletin*, 5 (2/3), Summer/Autumn: 15-17

Hartley D (1998) Repeat prescription; the national curriculum for initial teacher training, *British Journal of Educational Studies*, 46 (1), March: 68-83

Hartley J (2000) Letter. *Radio Times*, 25 November-1 December

Helsby G (1995) Teachers' Construction of Professionalism in England in the 1990s, *Journal of Education for Teaching*, 21 (3): 317-332

Hill M (2004) sound off, *Report*, March

House of Commons, Session 1999-2000, Education and Employment Committee (Education Sub-Committee) General Teaching Council. *Minutes of Evidence*, 9 February, 2000. London: The Stationery Office

Howard T (2001) A touch of classroom, *Time Out*, March 21-28

Howson J (2001) Young ones multiply, *Times Educational Supplement*, 9 November

http://www. tes.co.uk/have_your_say ..., 26/03/01

http://www. channel4.com/talk/pastchat, 29/04/01

Hughes P (1980) Pastoral Care: the historical context, in R Best, C Jarvis and P Ribbins (eds) *Perspectives on Pastoral Care*. London: Heinemann Organization in Schools series

Hutchings M, Menter I, Ross A, Thomson D, with Bedford D (2000) *Teacher Supply and Retention: a study of six London boroughs, 1998-9*. TTA Publications

Jacobs J (2001) Hospital Drama, in G Creeber (ed) *The Television Genre Book*. London: bfi Publishing

Jays D (2003) Mona Lisa Smile, *Sight and Sound*, 13 (3): 51

Jeffries S (2004) Must do better, *G2*, 18 February

Jenkins E (1997) First choice instead of last resort, *Times Educational Supplement*, 7 November

Jones K (1999) Representations 1969-80: notes on Kes and Grange Hill. Paper presented to History of Education Network at the European Conference on Educational Research, Lahti, Finland, 22-25 September, 1999

Jones T (1999) Letter. *Times Educational Supplement*, 10 December

Joseph J (2002) Review, *The Times*, 14 March

Judd J (1997) Stars help teacher recruitment, *Independent*, 15 October

Judd J (1999) Don't scorn the teaching 'Oscars', *Independent*, 15 July

Judd J (2004) final word, *Report*, January

Jury L (2004) Making History, with Bennett's Boys: public school drama rivals National Theatre greatest hits, *Independent*, 8 September

Kemp P (1996) *Sight and Sound*, 6 (5): 56

Kerckhoff A C, Fogelman K, Crook D and Reeder D (1996) *Going Comprehensive in England and Wales: A Study of Uneven Change*. London: The Woburn Press

Keroes J (1999) *Tales Out of School: Gender, Longing and the Teacher in Fiction and Film*. Southern Illinois: Southern Illinois University Press

Klein R (1997) A number crunched, *Times Educational Supplement*, 12 September

Kuhn A (1995) *Family Secrets*. London: Verso

Lacey N (1998) *Image and Representation (Key Concepts in Media Studies)*. London: Macmillan Press Ltd

Landesman C (1996) We don't need no education, *Sunday Times*, 12 May

Landy M (1991) *British Genres: Cinema and Society, 1930-1960*. Oxford NJ: Princetown University Press

Lawson M (2001) Mark Lawson on television, *G2*, 19 March

Lawton D (1994) *The Tory Mind on Education, 1979-94*. London: Falmer Press

Lee J (2004) Heads told to draft in WI, *Times Educational Supplement*, 19 November

Lindley D A (1993) *This Rough Magic: The Life of Teaching*. London: Bergin and Garvey

Lortie D C (1975) *Schoolteacher: A Sociological Study*. London: University of Chicago Press

Loukides P and Fuller L K (1990) *Beyond the Stars: Stock Characters in American Popular Film*. Bowling Green OH: Bowling Green State University Popular Press

Lowe R (1988) *Education in the Post-War Years: A Social History*. London: Routledge

Lowe R (1997) *Schooling and Social Change: 1964-1990*. London: Routledge

Maclaren P (1999) Silver screen dimmed by reality, *Times Educational Supplement*, 1 January

MacQueen A (2002) Learning Curves, *Big Issue*, 11-17 March

Maland C J (1988) The Social Problem Film, in W D Gehring (ed) *Handbook of American Film Genres*. London: Greenwood Press

Maltby R and Craven I (1995) *Hollywood Cinema: An Introduction*. Oxford: Blackwell

Mansell W (2001) Union move to push Puttnam out of office, *Times Educational Supplement*, 22 June

Mansell W and Dean C (2000) Most GTC seats held by teachers, *Times Educational Supplement*, 7 July

Mansell W, Dean C and Thornton K (2000) £10m recruiting campaign flops, *Times Educational Supplement*, 2 June

Mansell W, Learner S and Revell P (2001) Unions warn of £200m pay gap, *Times Educational Supplement*, 14 December

Mardle G and Walker M (1980) Strategies and Structure: Some Critical Notes on Teacher Socialisation, in P Woods (ed) *Teacher Strategies: Explorations in the Sociology of the School*. London: Croom Helm

Marland M (1989) *The Tutor and the Tutor Group: Developing your role as a Tutor.* Harlow: Longman (Longman Tutorial Resources)

Martin A (1984) Teacher, I Need You, *Metro Magazine:* 9-13

McCulloch G and Richardson W (2000) *Historical Research in Educational Settings.* Buckingham: Open University Press

McCulloch G (2001) The reinvention of teacher professionalism, in R Phillips and J Furlong (eds) *Education, Reform and the State: 25 years of politics, policy and practice.* London: Routledge/Falmer

McCulloch G (2004) Put theory into practice, *Times Educational Supplement,* 29 October

McGavin H (1995) Imagine all the pupils on Channel 4, *Times Educational Supplement,* 3 March

McLelland V A (1996) Quality and Initial Teacher Education, in VA McLelland and V Varma (eds) *The Needs of Teachers. London: Cassell*

McManus J (2000) Letter. *Times Educational Supplement,* 2 June

McManus M (1996) The Need to Maintain Morale: A Moral Issue, in VA McLelland and V Varma (eds) *The Needs of Teachers.* London: Cassell

McNeill P (1990) *Research methods.* London: Routledge

Measor L (1985) Critical Incidents in the Classroom: Identities, Choices and Careers, in S J Ball and I F Goodson (eds) *Teachers' Lives and Careers.* London: Falmer Press

Mitchell C and Weber S (1999) *Reinventing Ourselves as Teachers: Beyond Nostalgia.* London: Falmer Press

Moffitt J (1955) 'Blackboard Jungle' shock juvenile delinquency film, *Hollywood Reporter:* 3

Mooney (1998) Teachers take centre stage, *Guardian Education,* 8 December

Moore A (2004) *The Good Teacher: Dominant discourses in teaching and teacher education.* London: Routledge/Falmer

Moriarty H (1998) A no-win situation, *Guardian,* 14 July

Morley D (1980) *The 'Nationwide' Audience.* London: British Film Institute

Morley D (1992) *Television, Audiences and Cultural Studies.* London: Routledge

Mourby A (2002) Fantasy Teacher, *Times Educational Supplement,* 11 January

Mourby A (2002) Fantasy Teacher, *Times Educational Supplement,* 8 February

Murray L (1995) Personal and Social Education and Compulsory Requirements for Initial Teacher Education, *Pastoral Care,* December: 11-15

Myers N (1970) *Morning Star,* 14 October

Nicoll R (1996) Teachers' pests, *G2,* 19 September

Office for National Statistics (2000) *Social Trends 30.* London: The Stationery Office

O'Leary J (1997) Stars spearhead campaign for good teachers, *The Times,* October 15

Orr D (2001) The fantastic drama of the public sector, *Independent Review,* 20 March

Parker S (1997) *Reflective Teaching in the Postmodern World: A Manifesto for Education in Postmodernity.* Buckingham: Open University Press

Passmore B (2003) Call me Mr Forgettable, *Times Educational Supplement,* 19-26 December

Paton G (2004) Adverts target shortage subjects, *Times Educational Supplement*, 3 September

'Pay better teachers more', Editorial. *Guardian*, 22 April, 2000

Pearson A (1995) Hard labour at the chalkface, *Independent 2*, February 19

Phillips M (1996) *All Must Have Prizes*. London: Little Brown and Company (UK)

Phillips R (2001) Education, the state and the politics of reform: the historical context, 1976-2001, in R Phillips and J Furlong (eds) *Education, Reform and the State: 25 years of politics, policy and practice*. London: Routledge/Falmer

Plummer K (1990) (re-issue) *Documents of Life: An Introduction to the Problem and Literature of a Humanistic Methodology*. London: Unwin Hyman

Poitier S (2000) *The Measure of a Man: a memoir*. London: Pocket Books

Purves L (1999) Hope without the old humour, *Times Educational Supplement*, 16 July

Puttnam D (1999) Rewards for social heroes, *Times Educational Supplement*, 9 July

Puttnam D (2004) A time for innovation and celebration, *Education Guardian*, 26 October

Quinn A (2004) Mona Lisa Smile, *Independent*, 12 March

Rayner J (1998) *The Films of Peter Weir*. London: Cassell

Regan C and Regan B (1996) Teacher Trade Unionism in the 1990s: Problems and Strategies, in R Hatcher and K Jones (eds) *Education After The Conservatives: The response to the new agenda of reform*. Stoke on Trent: Trentham Books

Revell P (2002) An inspector leaves with glowing report, *Times Educational Supplement*, 1 March

Revell P (2002) New model army, *Guardian*, 23 October

Richards D (2004) Who sweeps the floor? *Church Times*, 11 June

Richardson R (2002) *In Praise of Teachers: Identity, Equality and Education (six topical lectures)*. Stoke on Trent: Trentham Books

Robey T (2004) Mona Lisa Smile, *Daily Telegraph*, 12 March

Robinson D (1959) *Financial Times*, 7 September

Rynning R (1996) Dangerous Liaisons, *Film Review*, February: 12-13

Schools and the Media, Queen Elizabeth II Conference Centre, Westminster, London, 30 November, 1998

Schwartz J (1960) The Portrayal of Educators in Motion Pictures, 1950-58, *The Journal of Educational Sociology: A Magazine of Theory and Practice*, 34(2): 82-9

Shaw M (2004) The really useful teacher channel, *Times Educational Supplement*, 13 February

Sheldon J (1986) Mastermind of Clockwise, *Mail on Sunday*, 30 March

'Shocking Film Of American Delinquency', *Daily Telegraph*, 13 September, 1955

Shorter E (1961) Modern Issues of School Life: Teacher's Story in Forthright Film, *Daily Telegraph*, 16 May

Sikes P, Measor L and Woods P (1985) *Teacher Careers: crises and continuities*. Lewes: Falmer Press

Simon B (1991) *Education and the Social Order, 1940-1990 (British Education since 1944)*. London: Lawrence and Wishart

Simon B (1994) *The State and Educational Change: Essays in the History of Education and Pedagogy.* London: Lawrence and Wishart

Smith A (1998) Time for a change of heart, *Times Educational Supplement,* 13 November

Smithers R (2001) Class notes, *Guardian Education,* 3 July

Smithers R (2001) Teachers on TV 'shown as idle drunks', *Guardian,* 3 August

Smithers R (2003) Lining up to protest, *Guardian Education,* 8 April

Smithers R (2004) MPs call for changes to teachers' pay, *Guardian,* 20 September

Smithers R (2004) Teaching in 1960s crackers, says inspector, *Guardian,* 6 October

Spare the Rod, *Monthly Film Bulletin,* July 1961: 96

Spare the Rod, *The Times,* 18/05/61

Spark M (2004) The real Miss Jean Brodie, *Radio Times,* 31 July-6 August

Squires G (1999) *Teaching as a Professional Discipline.* London: Falmer Press

Stacey J (1994) *Star Gazing: Hollywood cinema and female spectatorship.* London: Routledge

Staples T (1987) National Film Theatre Programme Notes, 31 August

Steen K E (1998) Cinema verité, *The Guide,* 7-13 March

Stein E (2004) All Girls Together, *The Eye,* 6 March

Stevenson N (1995) *Understanding Media Cultures: Social Theory and Mass Communication.* London: Sage Publications

Stewart W (2004) Merit pay for all teachers, *Times Educational Supplement,* 19 March

Stewart W (2004) Thousands may miss out on merit pay rises, *Times Educational Supplement,* 20 August

Stewart W and Shaw M (2004) Super-size class plans, *Times Educational Supplement,* 20 February

Street S (1997) *British National Cinema.* London: Routledge

Stubbs M (2003) *Ahead of the Class.* London: John Murray

Sutton A, Wortley A, Harrison J and Wise C (2000) Superteachers: From Policy Towards Practice, *British Journal of Educational Studies,* 48 (4), December: 413-428

Sweeting A (1999) Last night's TV, *G2,* 23 June

Taylor H (1989) *Scarlett's Women: 'Gone With The Wind' and its Female Fans.* London: Virago

Teachers, *The Guide,* 9-15 August, 2003

TES Diary, 15 August, 2003

Tester N (2000) A job for life? *Report,* March

The Teaching Awards Trust, 19 October, 2004

The Teaching Awards, 24 October, 2004

Thornton K (2000) Teaching adverts to appeal to 'thinkers', *Times Educational Supplement,* 27 October

Thornton K and Pyke N (2003) Wanted: selfish teachers, *Times Educational Supplement,* 22 August

Timmins N (1995) *The five giants: A Biography of the Welfare State.* London: Fontana Press

To-day's Cinema, volume 86, 31 May, 1956: 12

Tomlinson S (2001) *Education in a post-welfare society*. Buckingham: Open University Press

Toynbee P (2001) Opinion, *Radio Times*, 17-23 March

Trend R (1997) *Qualified Teacher Status: A Practical Introduction*. London: Letts Educational

Trewin J C (1968) *Robert Donat: A Biography*. London: William Heinemann Ltd

Tweedle J (1974) 'What Century is This, Miss?', *Guardian*, 9 December

Underwood S F (1992) *A Study of the Ideal Teacher: Heroic Metaphors of Teacher in Popular Literature*, The University of North Carolina at Greensboro (EdD)

Variety, 2 September, 1959

Viner B (1995) *Mail on Sunday*, 19 February

Viner C (2004) Short sharp shock, *Education Guardian*, 17 February

von Gunden K (1990) The College Professor in American Film, in P Loukides and L K Fuller *Beyond the Stars: Stock Characters in American Popular Film*. Bowling Green OH: Bowling Green State University Popular Press

Waller W (1932) *The Sociology of Teaching*. London: John Wiley

Walters M (1988) *Listener*, 120 (3089), 17 November: 39

Warburton T (1998) Cartoons and Teachers: Mediated Visual Images as Data, in J Prosser (ed) *Image-Based Research: A Sourcebook for Qualitative Researchers*. London: Falmer Press

Ward L (2003) Makeover show tops bill on TV channel for teachers, *Guardian*, 25 November

Warren G (2000) A vocation? Get lost! *Times Educational Supplement*, 5 May

Weber S and Mitchell C (1995) *That's funny, you don't look like a teacher! Interrogating Images and Identity in Popular Culture*. London: The Falmer Press

Weinstein P B (1998) *The Practice and Ideals of Education as Portrayed in American Films, 1939-1989*, Ohio University (PhD)

Whitwham I (2000) Don't mention the ..., *TES Friday*, 9 June

Who goes where, *Times Educational Supplement*, 24 March, 2000

Wilkin M (1996) *Initial Teacher Training: The Dialogue of Ideology and Culture*. London: Falmer Press

Williams E (1995) Cynic's guide to the inner-city burn-out cases, *Times Educational Supplement*, 10 February

Williams E (1999) Beasts that stalk the staffroom, *TES Friday*, 8 January

Williams Z (2003) Things you only know if you're not at work, *Guardian Weekend*, 15 February

Wilson C (2001) Why education is my chariot of fire, *Teachers*, July: 14-15

Wintour P and Watt N (2002) Morris quits: 'I've not done as well as I should have', *Guardian*, 24 October

Woods P (1995) *Teaching: Block 3, Unit 2, EU208, Education: a second-level course*. Milton Keynes: The Open University

Woods P and Jeffrey B (1998) Choosing Positions: living the contradictions of Ofsted, *British Journal of Sociology of Education*, 19 (4): 547-570

Woodward W (2001) Teaching not always a career for life, says Morris, *Guardian*, 12 June

Woodward W (2001) Fast learner, *Guardian Education*, 12 June

Woodward W (2001) Teachers steal the show, *Guardian Education*, 6 November

Worsley K (1998) Teachers burn their inspection grades, *Times Educational Supplement*, 22 May

Wragg E C and Wood E K (1994) Teachers' first encounters with their classes, in R Moon and A Shelton Mayes (eds) *Teaching and Learning in the Secondary School.* London: Routledge, in association with The Open University

Wragg E (1999) To Sir ... with scepticism, *Times Educational Supplement*, 9 July

Wragg E (2001) Time to rat on TV's teacher prat, *Times Educational Supplement*, 16 April

Wrathnall J (1988) *City Limits*, number 372, November 17-24: 27-28

Index

Mr Adams 6
Advanced Skills Teachers 28
advertising (*see* recruitment) 38, 42-44
Ahead of the Class 29, 132
Miss Allcock 6
Anderson, Todd 73, 111

Baker, Mike 13, 29, 38, 84
Mr Bean 6
Bell, David 12,18
Ben 36, 37
Betty 83
Blackboard Jungle 4, 36, 39, 62-64, 66, 81, 85, 96-99, 127, 133
Bob 36, 119
Brian 34, 35, 36
Brodie, Jean 68-70, 79, 82, 107, 109, 114-117
Brooks, Richard 63, 81
Bruce, Neil 29-30

Campbell, John 73,113
Carry on Teacher 1, 5, 6-8, 19
Casey, Simon 33, 34, 38, 109, 117-123, 125
charismatic teacher film and four-fold typology

eccentric 1, 19
enduring 39, 44, 59
resilient 61, 63, 67, 79, 85, 103-107
romantic 107, 109, 116, 124
Mr Chipping/Chips 39, 44-45, 46, 51, 52-53, 54, 55, 57, 59, 79
Circular 10/65 8, 9
classrooms 22, 45, 47, 62, 64-65, 66-67, 68-69, 71, 73, 75-76, 77-78, 79-80, 82, 86-87, 92-93, 94, 101-102, 110, 111, 117-118, 120-121
Clinty 95
Clockwise 2, 14-15, 19, 21
Connie 83
Croft, Michael 64, 66
Cromwell, Morris 10
Crossland, Anthony 8-9

Dadier, Richard 61, 62-64, 75, 96-99, 107
Dalton, Charlie 73, 110, 111
Damien 36
Dangerous Minds 25, 36, 74-77, 79, 81, 85, 99-103, 105, 131
Dare, Pamela 67, 77, 93, 94

Dawson, Peter 14
Dead Poets Society 22, 24, 36, 72-74, 107, 109-113, 117, 130
Mr Dingle 4-5, 19
Donat, Robert 39, 44, 131

Education Acts
1944 1, 2, 8
1988 2, 15, 16, 128
Ellis, Katherine 52-53
Eltham Green Comprehensive School 14
Emilio 75, 76
Escalante, Jaime 68, 70-72, 86-91, 107, 129
Evie 78
Ewan 36, 37
Ewell, Doris 10
examinations 2, 9, 90
Excellent Teachers' Scheme 28
extra-curricular activities 4, 115-116

Fallon, Jane 34, 37
Faraday High School 12
film
biographical 39, 44, 52
comedy 1, 19
social problem 85
Mr Frome 4-5
Fry, Stephen 50, 51, 131

Gannon, Lucy 30, 31
Garfield, Trevor 79-81
General Teaching Council 48-49
George, Ian 29-31, 37
Giselle 83
Goodbye, Mr Chips 36, 39, 44-45, 52-53, 57, 131
Goodbye, Mr Chips (television) 131
government
    Conservative 12-13, 15-16, 21, 24
    Labour 8
    New Labour 21, 24-28, 32-33, 56
Mr Grandy 101, 102-103
Green Paper 25-27
Mr Gregory 65
Griffith 75-76, 77, 103

The Happiest Days of Your Life 4
Hargreaves, A and four ages of teacher professionalism
    pre 1, 2, 19
    autonomous 2, 8, 19
    collegial 2, 13, 19
    post/postmodern 2, 16-17, 20
Harkness 65
Hearts and Minds 21-23, 37-38
Hedges, Bernard 10-11, 19
Henry, Lenny 29, 30
Hilton, James 39, 44
History Boys, The 132
Holland, Glenn 39-40, 45, 46-48, 53-54, 58-59
Holland, Iris 46, 54
Hope and Glory 21, 28-31, 37-38
Hunter, Evan 62, 63

Initial Teacher Training 1, 21, 40-41, 61

inspection (see also Ofsted) 5, 7-8, 23, 31
It's Great to be Young 1, 3, 4-5, 19

Mrs Jacobs 46, 47, 53
Mr Jenkins 64, 65
Jenny (in The Prime of Miss Jean Brodie) 68, 115
Jenny (in Teachers) 34, 35, 117, 118, 120
Jeremy 118
Joan 83
Johnson, LouAnne 75-77, 99-103, 107

Keating, John 36, 68, 72-74, 82, 107, 109, 114, 124
Kelly, Ruth 33
Kurt 34, 35, 36
Lincoln, Andrew 34

Lindsay 35, 36, 37
Lloyd, Teddy 114, 117
Lowther, Mr 114, 115-116

Matt 35, 36
Mr McAllister 73, 110, 112
McGovern, Jimmy 21
McGregor, Mary 68-69, 70, 115
Miss McKay 69, 70, 115-116
McKenzie, Drew 21-23, 37
Meister, Bill 46, 54, 58
Miller 62, 63, 97, 99
Mr Milton 6
Mr Holland's Opus 39-40, 45-48, 53-54, 58-59
Mr Molina 90
Monica 68, 69, 115
Mona Lisa Smile 82-84, 117, 131, 133
Murdoch, Jim 97, 98, 99

national curriculum 15, 105, 114, 127
Nolan, Mr 112

Ofsted 2, 17-18, 31, 37
Olmos, Edward James 71
187 79-81, 117
'Oscars' 48, 49-51, 132

parental involvement 67, 72, 74, 109, 124, 129
pastoral care 84, 88, 91-92, 97, 112, 118-119
Pegg, Babs 77, 94
Penny 35
performance related pay 26-28, 32
Perry, Neil 74, 110
personal/professional life balance 17, 22, 31, 33, 54, 59, 72, 85, 89, 101, 117, 128
Pfeiffer, Michelle 77, 131
Please Sir! 2, 9-11, 19
Poitier, Sidney 63, 66, 68
postmodern times 16, 17, 26, 54, 109
Price 10, 11
The Prime of Miss Jean Brodie 36, 68-70, 83-84, 109, 114-117, 131
private schooling 1, 2, 3-4, 8
Puttnam, Lord David 42, 48-49, 51, 55, 64
Dr Ralston 57

real teachers and
    autonomy 8, 9, 15
    compromise 17, 27
    demonisation 9, 11, 13, 15, 24, 88
    morale 24, 48
    status 8, 9, 24, 48, 127
reality level 90, 103-107, 113, 122, 126-131

recruitment 41, 44
reel teachers and
  aspiration to 111,
  113, 114
  born to teach 94,
  104
  cult of personality
  94, 100, 104, 106,
  112
  isolation 102, 103,
  112-113
  success rate 90, 91,
  98
retention 51
retirement 25, 58
Reynolds, Kevin 81
Roberts, Julia 132
routes into teaching
  Bachelor of
  Education 6, 13, 40
  Certificate of
  Education 13, 40
  Graduate Training
  Programme 41
  Postgraduate
  Certificate of
  Education 41
  Registered Training
  Programme 41
  School Centred
  Initial Teacher
  Training 41

Sandy 68, 115
Saunders, John 61, 64-
  66, 75
schooling
  elementary 2
  primary 2, 10, 12
  secondary
    comprehensive
    1, 2, 8-9, 11, 12,
    13, 14, 26
    grammar 1, 3,
    4, 8, 9, 13, 26
    modern 1, 3, 5,
    8, 9, 26
    technical 3, 8

senior management
  team/senior
  leadership team 84,
  95, 99, 101
  service (*see* vocation) 17,
  54
Short, Clare 132
Miss Short 6, 7
Smith, Maggie 114, 131
Smithy 10, 19
Southfields Community
  College 132
Spare the Rod 64-66
Stand and Deliver 68,
  70-72, 85, 86-91, 105
St Trinians series 4
Stubbs, Marie 29, 132
Mr Shotton 22, 23
staffrooms 96, 98-99
Stimpson, Brian 14-15,
  19, 99
streaming 10, 12
superhead 28
Susan 34, 35, 121

Teacher Training Agency
  41, 42, 43, 55
Teachers (C4 series) 21,
  33-37, 38, 56, 109,
  117-124, 125, 130
teaching and learning
  styles 3, 12, 84, 87,
  92, 100-101, 111, 117-
  118, 124
teaching life cycle
  early days 44-48
  mid-career 52-54
  latter days 56-59
teaching unions 15-16,
  49-50, 64
  NAHT 43, 49
  NAS/UWT 27
  NUT 24, 27, 32, 50
  PAT 34
Thackeray, Mark 61, 66-
  68, 77-79, 91-96, 107
Thatcher, Margaret 13,
  32

*Times Educational
  Supplement* 11, 25
Tom Brown's Schooldays
  131
Tomlinson, Mike 18
To Sir, With Love 22, 36,
  66-68, 77, 85, 91-96,
  105, 131
To Sir, With Love 2 77-79

vocation 26, 44, 46, 52,
  53, 55, 56, 59, 117

Mr Wakefield 6-8, 19, 99
Watson, Katherine 82-84
Welfare State 2, 5, 16
West 62, 63
Weston, Theo 95
William Tyndale primary
  school 12
Williams, Robin 73, 113,
  131
Wolters, Gene 47, 53
Woodhead, Chris 18, 24
workload agreement 21,
  32-33
Wragg, Ted 28, 30, 33,
  51, 61, 77